"*No Better Mom for the Job* is one of the most practical and applicable books for mothers today. You'll get more out of these pages than mere knowledge. You'll receive courage—courage to show up for this important job each day; courage to reach out and make friends and accept help; and courage to practice presence over perfection with your loved ones. This is a book you'll want to share with your friends, so grab an extra copy while you're at it!"

—Wendy Speake, coauthor of *Triggers* and *Parenting Scripts*, and author of *The 40-Day Sugar Fast*

"Becky is not only a gifted writer, but with *No Better Mom for the Job*, she tenderly and confidently teaches and affirms truths that embolden a flailing mother's heart. This book is a must-read for moms who are looking for that mentor-voice to speak wisdom into unsure places."

—Sarah Mae, author of *The Complicated Heart*

"Becky had me laughing and crying within minutes. She gracefully breathes courage into the souls of weary moms. I'll be gifting this book, a pack of diapers, and a box of tissues to every new mom I know."

—Anjuli Paschall, founder of The Moms We Love Club

"Becky Keife's heartfelt book is a reminder that the simplest acts leave the greatest impact. Her writing is tender and relatable, like a letter from a trusted friend. *No Better Mom for the Job* is delightful!"

—Jessica N. Turner, author of *The Fringe Hours* and *Stretched Too Thin*

"In *No Better Mom for the Job*, Becky Keife puts into words what every mom feels but few have the courage to confess. Then, like a wise friend, she offers a refreshing perspective and practical

D0047398

action steps to find peace, purpose, and confidence in being the very best mom for our job."

—Monica Swanson, author of *Boy Mom*

"Becky Keife gives the most beautiful life ring of hope to every mama waiting to feel adequate enough for motherhood. Her brave words, wrapped in truth, will inspire and encourage any woman in any season of motherhood. Every page is a wonder, inviting us to live in the present and embrace the children we each have been uniquely given, one simple step and one simple prayer at a time. There's beauty and hope for every mom."

—September McCarthy, author of *Why Motherhood Matters*

no better mom for the job

Parenting with Confidence
(Even When You Don't Feel Cut Out for It)

BECKY KEIFE

BETHANYHOUSE

a division of Baker Publishing Group
Minneapolis, Minnesota

© 2019 by Becky Keife

Published by Bethany House Publishers
11400 Hampshire Avenue South
Bloomington, Minnesota 55438
www.bethanyhouse.com

Bethany House Publishers is a division of
Baker Publishing Group, Grand Rapids, Michigan

Printed in the United States of America

ISBN 978-0-7642-3324-1

Library of Congress Control Number: 2019020802

Unless otherwise indicated, Scripture quotations are from the Holy Bible, New International Version. NIV®. Copyright © 1973, 1978, 1984, 2011 by Biblica, Inc.™ Used by permission of Zondervan. All rights reserved worldwide. www.zondervan.com

Scripture quotations identified CEV are from the Contemporary English Version © 1991, 1992, 1995 by American Bible Society. Used by permission.

Scripture quotations identified CSB from the Christian Standard Bible®, Copyright © 2017 by Holman Bible Publishers. Used by permission. Christian Standard Bible® and CSB® are federally registered trademarks of Holman Bible Publishers.

Scripture quotations identified ESV are from The Holy Bible, English Standard Version® (ESV®), copyright © 2001 by Crossway, a publishing ministry of Good News Publishers. Used by permission. All rights reserved. ESV Text Edition: 2011

Scripture quotations identified MSG are from THE MESSAGE. Copyright © by Eugene H. Peterson 1993, 1994, 1995, 1996, 2000, 2001, 2002. Used by permission of NavPress. All rights reserved. Represented by Tyndale House Publishers, Inc.

Scripture quotations identified NLT are from the Holy Bible, New Living Translation, copyright © 1996, 2004, 2015 by Tyndale House Foundation. Used by permission of Tyndale House Publishers, Inc., Carol Stream, Illinois 60188. All rights reserved.

Portions of chapter 4 appeared in two previous publications and are used by permission: The Gift of Friendship, edited by Dawn Camp (Revell, 2016), and A Moment to Breathe, edited by Denise Hughes (B&H Books, 2017).

Cover design by Emily Weigel; photo by Becky Keife

Author is represented by Books & Such Literary Agency.

19 20 21 22 23 24 25   7 6 5 4 3 2 1

In keeping with biblical principles of creation stewardship, Baker Publishing Group advocates the responsible use of our natural resources. As a member of the Green Press Initiative, our company uses recycled paper when possible. The text paper of this book is composed in part of post-consumer waste.

To Noah, Elias, and Jude

You are my greatest teachers
and my favorite treasures.
I love you every day.

Contents

Contents

Discussion guide available at
NoBetterMomBook.com

Foreword

I lay in bed last night exhausted and looked at the ceiling. Then I got back out again and briefly knelt down next to my bed with my face pressed into the mattress and mumbled a prayer.

God, here I am. I don't know what I'm doing.

Fourteen years into parenting and I often feel just as lost now as I did at the beginning. Our kids are toddling into middle and high school instead of just around our living room, and last night I realized, again, how vulnerable I am. How there are no guarantees and how I don't have all the answers.

Becky's book has been keeping me company the last few weeks. Literally. It's been in my computer bag, and then on my desk, and then next to my bed, and sometimes waiting for me next to a cup of lukewarm coffee. And last night her words came back to make sense of my pounding headache and the hamster wheel of doubt that was spinning in my head:

"Oh, Motherhood. You are breathtakingly beautiful and heart-breakingly brutal. You are the highest honor and greatest challenge I have ever been given. One minute you make me want to weep, and the next throw my head back and dance in a whirlwind of painful, extravagant grace. Since I don't dance in public, I guess stifled weeping over my steamy latte will have to do."

I've cried plenty the last decade plus. I've laughed and danced too. And I've borne witness to how fast whiny babies can grow up into sometimes even whinier teens. Last night after I'd cleaned my daughter's newly pierced ears and after the boys had showered and later when they were shaking out their blankets and crawling into beds, surrounded by the stuffed toys I hope they never surrender, they were little again. When they curled up their long legs and tucked their sinewy arms under their heads to sleep, I recognized them again. The familiar babies I held for hours through the shifts of nursing and burping.

I catch glimpses of those days in their growing faces.

They're caught in the in-between, and here I am trying to guide them, realizing I'm just as in-between as they are.

So I crawled back out of my own bed and planted my face in the mattress and didn't even ask for help. I just said, *Here I am.*

Here I am, God.

Please find me on your map.

Please find all of us.

I like to think of God with a giant "you are here" star marked on His beautiful map of infinite possibility.

I just needed to know last night that at least someone knew where we'd all end up.

Then I could crawl back under my own covers and it was enough. Knowing that I'm not alone. Or expected to know it all or have all the answers. I can't resolve all the conflict for my kids— especially not the kind that brews inside them. I can't always solve disputes with angry neighbors or teen boys who chase each other down the soccer field with frustrated yells.

Some nights all I can do is kneel down and say out loud all the things I can't do.

And then I heard Becky's voice, walking up beside the thoughts in my head like the good friend she is, saying, *That's OK. All the fallout from today and the unknowns of tomorrow don't get to change the fact that there actually is no better mom for the job of wrangling your kids than you.*

You're holding a guarantee in your hands right now, friend. In the pages of this book is all the guaranteed reassurance you will need to remind you that you can actually get through tomorrow and the day after that. And the toddler years and tweens and all the firsts and lasts that are still to come. And I know Becky knows because she invites us all into her own doubts and days of kids splashing around in puddles of their own pee. (I know!) She's a mom who loses her mind and fears she'll never find friendship or time to figure out who she is in this strange new land of motherhood. She doesn't hold back. She goes there. And she takes us with her so that we can all feel less afraid and less alone and more sure of ourselves despite the voices in our heads.

Because Becky believes that our "emptiness is not something to be ashamed of or quick-fixed. It's part of the motherhood gift—pointing you to Him."

Let this book be the words you need to fill your emptiness. Let it pour truth and courage into your bones. Let it lift you and hold you and comfort you on the nights you doubt yourself. And the days filled with do-overs. Because it's honest and relatable. Because who doesn't love a mom who admits her limits in the kitchen but boasts of her "robust stamina for card games" and "squirrel kisses." I have no idea what the latter is, but it made me laugh out loud and want to learn more from this fellow mom who isn't afraid of my failures and is convinced, beyond all the voices in my own head, that I am capable. Go ahead, turn the page, and let her convince you too.

—Lisa-Jo Baker,
author of *The Middle Matters* and *Surprised by Motherhood*,
co-host of the *Out of the Ordinary* podcast, and mom
to three very loud kids. From her dining room table,
just outside of Washington, DC.

Introduction

You Were Made for This

I wish I could remember exactly when the thought first entered my mind. The fog of time makes the details fuzzy—a mental haze only mothers well acquainted with years of sleep deprivation would understand. It could have been after a brutal nap strike or car seat–buckling meltdown or another failed attempt at a seemingly simple library outing—*how hard can it be to sit and listen to the nice lady read the nice story without climbing on the furniture and breaking a chair?* It could have been any one of a million ordinary moments, or likely their culmination, that led to the thought I never expected to have as a young mom: *There is something wrong with my child or there is something wrong with me; either way, we are definitely not a match.*

The thought felt like an itchy sweater two sizes too small that I was doomed to wear forever. It rubbed my heart raw.

You see, I loved my son. I loved his blond ringlets and fiercely tight hugs. I loved the way he galloped around the yard like a little colt, the way his eyes lit up over dragonflies and kitty cats, the way he nuzzled in the crook of my neck, his chest beating against mine.

I loved my tiny tot. But many days—most days—I felt totally ill-equipped to be his mom. For such a little person, Noah was *a lot.* The gap between what he needed and what I had to give was big. How could I possibly find a bridge?

I used to think I was the only one who felt this way. All the other moms with stylish yoga pants and curled eyelashes and kids with matching socks and tamed locks didn't seem to struggle the way I did. Everyone else seemed to be able to cook dinner and take a shower and leave the park without a shoeless child heaved over their shoulder like a flailing, wailing sack of potatoes. I used to think it was just my boy—spirited and strong-willed to his core. Or that the problem was *me*—a mom who was somehow not strong enough or consistent enough, not patient enough or clever enough to avoid negotiating with my toddler like he was a skilled lawyer.

I thought that if I had a different kid or my kid had a different mom, things would be different. I would *feel* different.

Fast-forward a decade and add two more boys. Now, as a semi-seasoned mom of three, I can tell you that even with different kids who have different personalities and temperaments, the same struggle exists, which leads to the same fundamental questions: Do I believe I'm the right mom for my child? Or do I believe God made a mistake in pairing us together?

Though each of our motherhood stories is unique—no two mamas have walked, crawled, or stumbled down the exact same road—I believe we all share the common bond of feeling like we're not quite cut out for the job. It's a fear that transcends our individual challenges and abilities. Whether you birthed your child through hours of physical labor or you labored through years of prayer and paperwork for a courtroom declaration, at some point every mom wonders if she really is enough. Our feelings of inadequacy may manifest in different ways, but essentially, we're all grappling with the same thing: how to love well the imperfect child entrusted to our imperfect care.

We're all grappling with the same thing: how to *love* well the imperfect child *entrusted* to our imperfect care.

How do we discipline, challenge, and encourage them? How do we teach and train with wisdom and grace all the livelong day? How do we love, champion, protect, and provide from dawn till dusk—with early-morning risers and late-night crib-climbers who have a thousand needs, ask a million questions, and push every boundary—without losing our ever-lovin' mind? How do we understand a child who is so unlike us, or better—and harder—yet, love the one in whom we see our own glaring reflection? How do we train them up in the way they should go when we are stumbling to find our own way?

If you're nodding along in bewildered agreement and waiting for me to get to the part where I tell you I've figured out all the answers and here's your ten-step solution to total-confidence parenting . . . I guess now's the time to break the news that this is not a book of magical motherhood how-to's and inadequacy quick fixes. I don't have it all figured out. But I know the One who does. And I want to virtually reach through these pages, put my arm around your shoulders that are sagging under the weight of motherhood, and whisper in your ear, *You can do this. You ARE doing it. God did not make a mistake in pairing you and your child together. You are the right mom for the job!*

A Welcomed Invitation

I'll admit that in the thick of motherhood, it can be easy to forget that Jesus is the One I really need. In my "at a loss, don't know what to do, don't know how to fix this" moments (please tell me you have them too!), I was quick to reach for expert advice from a parenting book, or the nearest bag of Fritos. Surely *someone* knows why my kid won't sleep or won't stop lying, why I love my littles but I can't stop crying. Surely a salty snack will curb my hunger to be understood, calm my temper, or curtail my frustration.

There's nothing wrong with chips or practical help. But I needed to understand that my desperate desire to be a good mom was *not* an indication of my deficit as a parent; it was a soul-alert that I had an invitation awaiting my acceptance. Ding ding. Notification! There's an outstanding offer of help from the One who made you a mother.

God was inviting me to walk through motherhood with Him. And that didn't mean adding one more thing to my teetering, over-loaded plate. It meant that He wanted to carry it for me and heap on piles of wisdom, patience, love, and grace.

He wanted to join me on the floor playing Legos and cheer me on when I figured out one more way to cook chicken. It meant He wanted to be my teacher and help me learn the landscape of my children so I could understand how they're created, how our strengths and weaknesses can work together. Jesus was there to be my friend and celebrate every motherhood victory with me—*potty training, learning to read, didn't burn the grilled cheese!* And He also was ready to hug my heart tight with every motherhood ache—*uncertain diagnosis, repeated bad habits, will they ever listen?*

He wants to be there for all of it.

All I had to do was accept His invitation.

I responded with a prayer: *God, I don't believe You made a mistake in making me my kids' mom. Even on days I feel inadequate, I believe You have called me to this role and that You are willing and able to equip me to be the mom my children need. Please walk this motherhood road with me.*

I didn't pray this once or twice. I prayed it day after day. My feelings about myself as a mom were fickle. I needed to be covered by the truth.

This prayer was the beginning of transforming my motherhood story. From buckling under the weight of discontentment to growing in gratitude. From floundering alone to thriving in friendship. From believing that my kids would be better off with someone else to embracing that I'm the right mom for the job. From drowning in my own inadequacy to parenting with confidence.

Turns out, there wasn't something wrong with my son or something wrong with me. There was something right with Jesus.

A Match Made in Heaven

As you read the chapters ahead, I hope you will see that confidence does not come from always knowing (or doing) the right thing. It's not about having the perfect response for every meltdown or back talk or challenging parenting moment. It's not about being 100 percent prepared for every stage your child will go through. Parenting with confidence does not mean having every child-rearing philosophy memorized, every parenting technique mastered. That's way too much pressure! When I think of parenting with confidence in those terms, my inadequacy meter skyrockets to red: DANGER, DANGER, YOU WILL NEVER GET THIS MOTHERING JOB RIGHT.

No! Ixnay that kind of thinking. Throw the notion that confident parenting equals perfect parenting out with the diaper pail and moldy banana peel you found wedged under the couch. Parenting with confidence means remembering that God did not make a mistake in making you your kid's mom. Parenting with confidence means leaning on the never-ending grace and forgiveness found in Jesus Christ alone. Confident parenting means asking the Spirit of God to empower you day by day, moment by moment to love, train, and raise your kids well—trusting that He will do it. And when you falter or fail and don't know what to say or do or how to keep on keeping on, you believe that the God who loves your kids even more than you do will fill in the gaps for what you lack, and tomorrow will bring mercies anew.

In other words, parenting with confidence (even when you don't feel cut out for it) means having confidence that

1. God matched you and your child up on purpose.
2. God is your greatest partner, cheerleader, and champion in motherhood.
3. God sees you, He goes with you, and He will equip you.

Whether you're a new mom or have a decade or more of parenting under your belt, your journey isn't over. Let this book be a companion of encouragement on this stretch of the road. Through these pages, you'll learn how to bridge that impassible gap between your own inadequacy and what your child needs. I have so many practical tips and strategies I can't wait to share with you! But what I'm most excited about is helping you see that the primary bridge every mom needs to fill her gaps is actually a Person.

I have never known my deep need for Jesus or the depth of His love for me like I have as a mother. He is the bridge between the end of my rope and the beginning of grace.

Friend, these are the long and trying, precious time–flying days. Days that make our eyes well with tears and hearts swell with pride at the joy of being Mama, raising the ones entrusted to our care. Days that try our patience, test our resolve, and sometimes make us want to shake our fist because being a mom can be plain hair-pulling hard. Rather than spinning our wheels to make these days slow down or speed up, we need the right guide to walk with us. We need Someone to take our hand along this beauty-soaked, soul-stretching road of motherhood, to lead us and equip us. Day by day, moment by moment.

I know the Guide. I'm hoping you do too. If not, I want to introduce you.

one

You Just Don't Seem Happy Anymore

Five years ago on a Wednesday night, I sat in a circle of moms in mismatched chairs. I was at a small church back in my hometown, but I didn't know any of the women snacking on chocolate-covered Rice Krispie Treats except the one who invited me to speak. After coffee from Styrofoam cups and an awkward icebreaker, it was my turn to share the message. I was excited to tell these mamas about joy! About how giving thanks is the key to the full life promised in Christ. But before I got to the full-of-life part, I first had to tell them about being empty.

I took a deep breath and told the story of that night at my kitchen sink. How in the midst of my scrubbing burnt cheese off dinner dishes, my husband made the comment that changed everything.

"You just don't seem happy anymore," he said.

My soapy hands stalled.

It wasn't an accusation or a put-down. Chris wasn't mad. It was more of an observation that made him sad. I was caught off guard. *How could he say that?* I mean, I was a pretty positive person. I laughed throughout the day at my trifecta of tiny testosteronies, as I liked to call my three young boys. People often told me I had a great smile. I often told people how my life was so blessed. *There's plenty of happy in this house, mister.* And to top it all off, I had been reading the book of James. The famous words of the half brother of Jesus were etched on my heart: "Count it all joy" (James 1:2 ESV).

So why would Chris say that? I wanted to defend myself. I wanted to refute his statement and spew out all the reasons he was wrong. But instead of being defensive, the Holy Spirit urged me to be reflective.

"I hear you," I finally said.

I held the rest of the words that wanted to spill out and let Chris's statement scrub the rough places in my heart.

As I considered the incident over the days and weeks that followed, I had to admit that my husband was right. I really wasn't happy. More than that, my life was lacking joy. When I got raw and honest with myself, I saw what Chris saw; I was a stressed-out mess hanging on by a grumbling thread. I acted like a quasi-victim of my own life. I was living like the honor of being mama to three small children was a never-ending trial instead of a gift. Like the sleepless nights and squeezed budget and raging hormones from being pregnant or nursing for five years straight were all happening *to me.* And I felt powerless to do anything but suffer through it.

My problem wasn't Noah, my firstborn, or Elias, who came nineteen months later, or Jude, who crashed onto the scene twenty-two short months after that. My problem wasn't the diaper blowouts or the creaky halls and tight walls of our two-bedroom rental house. It wasn't missing my old job or struggling under the weight of caring for littles while working from home. The root of my problem was ingratitude. Somehow, I knew it deeply.

But I *was* grateful. Wasn't I? Every night I thanked God for healthy babies and food to feed them. I was thankful that Chris had a good job and short commute. I was thankful I got to choose to stay home with my children. Thankful I could work from my dining room table to help provide for my family. These were privileges not every mom got, and I didn't take them for granted. So how had ingratitude taken root in my heart when gratitude was easy to profess on the surface?

I asked God to show me the source of my ungratefulness. I felt a question emerge in my spirit. *What do you spend your energy thinking about?* Well, for starters, I think about how to synchronize nap schedules, what on earth am I going to make for dinner, and when was the last time I washed my hair?

Dig deeper.

Okay then. I pushed through the mama brain fog and past the easy answers. I started to take note of my inner dialogue. Not the active thoughts about the parenting dilemma I wanted to solve or what fun family thing were we going to do Saturday afternoon; I listened closely to the passive thoughts that rose from my subconscious. Soon I came to recognize a familiar tape that played poor-me melodies on repeat. The soundtrack was subtle. But it was there.

The voice inside my head whispered this life of mine was just too much for anyone to handle. The laundry and dishes that were never done despite my perpetual doing. Three active boys who constantly needed to run, play, eat, bathe—needing every part of me. And the part-time job I couldn't give up so we could make it through to the end of each month. I ached for time with God, time with my husband, and but a moment for myself. Time to scrape that mystery muck off the refrigerator shelf. The dissonant song in my mind whined that there was never enough time for it all. And how could there ever be enough time to do extra things like celebrate a friend, help a neighbor, pursue a dream, or remove the green crayon marks marring the white walls, when I simply struggled to make dinner while not losing my temper and keeping my three monkeys out of their make-believe trees? *Thud.*

"Noah, stop jumping off your dresser!"

Now, you've got to know I didn't bemoan these thoughts to everyone. I wasn't an outright complainer. But my ingratitude did slip out. It seeped out in the long sigh that immediately followed whenever someone asked, *How are you doing, Becky?* It leaked out with every comment about how tired or busy or worn-out I was by my crazy boy crew, which was the precursor to any positive thing I might say. I started to realize that each wayward sigh I made was a sideways means of seeking affirmation. I wanted someone to understand, to acknowledge the challenges I faced each day. I wanted someone to see all the unseen effort I put forth to keep a small herd of littles thriving, or at least surviving.

I knew I wasn't the only hardworking mom. Yet, I felt . . . overlooked.

The tape in my head and sighs slipping out weren't the only indications of my ingratitude. Each day I saved spewing all the poor-me sewage for someone: my husband. Just moments after Chris walked through the door, I felt compelled to download the grievances of my day. Every tantrum, back talk, and time-out. Every less than terrific mothering moment that made me want to pull my hair out, he had to hear.

No wonder he thought I wasn't happy.

I knew my husband believed I was a good mom. I knew he realized motherhood wasn't easy. But still I wanted more. More affirmation. More validation. More shiny gold stars to show that I made it through even when it was hard. Somehow I thought the way to get that was by making sure he knew that it was hard.

Retraining Your Focus

Have you been there, friend? Aching under the tension of loving the ones who call you mama yet longing for an escape from them? Feeling stretched by the tension of the blessings you know and the discontentment you feel?

Shortly after the "you don't seem happy anymore" comment, I started reading *One Thousand Gifts* by Ann Voskamp. Her words from the opening chapter confirmed what convicted my heart: "Satan's sin becomes the first sin of all humanity: the sin of ingratitude. Adam and Eve are, simply, painfully, ungrateful for what God gave. Isn't that the catalyst of all my sins? Our fall was, has always been, and always will be, that we aren't satisfied in God and what he gives. We hunger for something more, something other."*

I was sincerely thankful for my children, my husband, and home. Truly grateful for God's provision of work and finances. Yet my focus was still fixed on my lack. Lack of sleep, affirmation, and personal space. Lack of time to meet all the needs of my family and have half an ounce of energy left over for me. But Ann, a farmer's wife and mom of six, zeroed in on the real root of my issue: "The real problem of life is never a lack of time. The real problem of life—*in my life*—is lack of thanksgiving."†

Bingo.

As a floundering mama with bags under my eyes big enough to prove my lack of sleep, I made a choice to stop fixating on a deficit I had no power to change. After all, God is pretty set on the whole twenty-four hours in a day thing. Instead, I decided to concentrate on what was fully within my grasp: my ability to give thanks.

I started to retrain my focus from what stressed me about being a mom to what blessed me.

The daily list of things that brought me joy raising three young boys was endless. Watching eyes shine with wonder over wiggly worms. Receiving a son's fierce love-hug. Fixing countless scraped knees with magical kisses. Listening to my boys say, "*I wuv you, brudder*" to one another. But unless I intentionally slowed to recognize the gifts—to name them—they slipped away into the haze of the day before truly being savored. Because the next hard thing

---

* Ann Voskamp, *One Thousand Gifts* (Grand Rapids, MI: Zondervan, 2011), 15.
† Ibid., 72.

in potty training or sibling-rivalry refereeing would crop up and crowd out the blessing. I had to learn to slow down and purposely thank God in the moment.

I've talked to enough moms over the years to know I'm not the only one who is in danger of getting swallowed by the mundane. I know the hidden struggle many of us have with discontentment—which breeds guilt and opens the door wide for feelings of inadequacy. If discontentment has seeped into your heart, it will undermine the gift it is to be a mother. It will drive a wedge between you and the One who wants to walk with you and equip you on your motherhood journey. So what do we do about it?

Start by identifying the tapes that play in your head. What do those inner-dialogue loops sound like for you? Take mental notes. Actually write it down if that helps you. Hold up what you're saying to yourself, about yourself, against what you know to be true. See if there are any disparities. For example, a common chorus of my internal dialogue went like this: *Motherhood will always be like this. I will never have enough time to get everything done. I feel like I'm drowning.*

I felt like the diaper days and sleepless nights would always be my motherhood reality. "The years fly by," people would say. There were no flying years in my experience. Yet when I really looked at that statement, *Motherhood will always be like this,* I knew it wasn't true. My boys were growing with each passing day, and no matter how long the hours between dinner and bedtime felt, the years with littles were a season, not a life sentence. Language of absolutes is rarely helpful. *Always* and *never* would best be lost in the dryer with all the random socks. And was I drowning? No, not literally. Was the feeling of overwhelm true to my experience? Often it was. But telling myself that my life was unmanageable and I wasn't cut out for the job wouldn't change my reality or help my mentality. It just made me sink deeper more quickly.

Whether what we're telling ourselves is fact or fiction, our mental soundtrack becomes an integral part of our motherhood story. What story do you want to live?

Language of absolutes is rarely helpful. *Always* and *never* would best be lost in the dryer with all the random socks.

We must learn to walk the fine line of being honest about the challenges of motherhood and breaking free from destructive negativity and a victim mentality. Now hear me, I don't believe anything good comes from slapping an Instagram filter and fake smile on our lives and pretending that every moment of motherhood is chocolate unicorn rainbows.

Motherhood is not all one thing.

It is not all joy, but it is certainly not all struggle and sorrow.

When I think about how stinking adorable and delicious my kids are, I wouldn't mind drizzling some caramel sauce over them with a sprinkle of sea salt and taking a big bite. (Is that weird? Of course, I'm kidding.) But along with the bursting love for my children that I can't contain comes a suffocating desperation that's hard to name. I feel the need to say it again: Motherhood is not all one thing. Maybe you need permission to claim that today.

I've known Jesus since I was a little girl, but nothing has rocked my spiritual journey and brought me to my knees in uncontrollable tears like being a mom.

I'm so thankful God can handle our raw, unfiltered responses. We don't have to shellac our feelings for His sake. In fact, admitting our unfineness is the first step to accepting how much we need Jesus. I can't be the right mom for my kids on my own. This life *is* too much for me to handle! But with God as my guide—when I allow Him to be my joy, my strength, my ever-present help—there's no better mom for my kids than me. This means learning to remain open with God and tender toward myself about my struggles, while rooting out the negative internal dialogue that threatens to keep me in a pit of self-pity.

It boils down to this: Stop rehearsing the hard.

The Antidote for Not-Enough

Whether one child demands your full attention or you're managing a household brimming with kids, whether you're a single mom, stepmom, or foster mom, girl mom or boy mom, a joyfully pregnant or pulling-out-your-hair mom, we will all experience the hard of motherhood. That's a given. But we don't have to rehearse it.

The hard comes easy. We need to rehearse, repeat, and rehash the good.

Start by naming your "not enough." Time is always first on my list. But some days it's patience, wisdom, or culinary creativity—*Yes, dear, we're having turkey chili. Again.* What is it for you? Your kid's behavior isn't good enough, your spouse isn't understanding or helpful enough, your home isn't big enough, your career isn't fulfilling enough, or maybe your friendships aren't deep enough. Whatever it is, identify the deficit you fixate on. Then, stop the "not enough" soundtrack by replacing it with songs of thanksgiving. Begin to give thanks for the *good* in what feels most *hard*. Sounds counterintuitive, but this is how gratitude grows deep roots.

In my longing for more time, I intentionally started to give thanks for the time I already had. Seeing the good turned into ordinary prayers of gratitude.

Thank You, God, for time to fold this load of laundry. Thank You for the family who gets to wear these clothes you've provided.

Thank You for these five minutes to let hot water beat on my back in the shower. Thank You that the kids are asleep and I can hear my own heartbeat.

Thank You for this hour to work while Noah and Elias are in school and Jude takes a nap. Thank You for the gift of time to focus on what's right in front of me and earn a paycheck.

The other day on Instagram my friend Jennifer put the point perfectly: "Gratitude is acknowledging the goodness in our lives as life exists today, *not as we wish it to be.*"

Say that thing you lack out loud—*time, affirmation, patience, sleep*—and decide today to look for ways to give thanks for it anyway. Training our hearts in the practice of gratitude doesn't diminish the hard; it opens us up to the fullness of the blessings we're already living.

29

On the heels of admitting my unhappiness, I made a conscious effort to notice the good in the ordinary. Making banana muffins with little helpers. Cardboard boxes turned into spaceships. Boys playing for fifteen contented minutes. Sidewalk chalk on concrete canvases. The way my toddler said "mo-lawn-er" when he really meant lawn mower. Couch cuddles under a fuzzy blanket. Hot tea to soothe a sore throat. Leftovers.

I counted each blessing as grace straight from God, jotting them down in a journal I got on clearance. The practice was a little awkward at first. Am I really going to write down squeezing a new tube of toothpaste, putting on socks fresh from the dryer, and a day without projectile spit-up on a list of things I'm thankful for? Why, yes I am. Because no matter how small or how fleeting, those were gifts, and by calling them out my joy and gratitude intensified. In the same way sleep begets sleep (we all know an overly tired toddler is nearly impossible to put to bed), so does gratitude spur on more gratitude. The circumstances of my days didn't change. I still had a lot to juggle as a full-time mom of three children under four while working part-time from home. But the attitude of my heart began to slowly transform through the thanks pouring from my pen and lips.

A sink of dirty dishes and my husband saying words I didn't want to hear was the gritty place my joy story started. I told those mamas gathered in the mismatched chairs the same thing I want to tell you: If you suffer from ingratitude like I did, you don't have to stay stuck there. Joy and contentment are yours for the choosing. No one has to stay empty.

You can start weeding out discontentment and growing roots of gratitude today. Grab yourself a journal. It doesn't have to be big or fancy. A yellow legal pad, a lined notebook from the Dollar Spot at Target, or the Hello Kitty diary your daughter never uses will do just fine. Like I did after reading Ann Voskamp's book, begin building the habit of recording your daily blessings. Don't see this as another thing to add to your overloaded plate. See it as a way to capture, savor, and appreciate the treasures that are already yours but might be overlooked.

Leave your journal open on the kitchen table and scratch each bit of thanks down as it unfolds. Or at the end of the day, when your beautiful, sassy, sticky, finicky kiddos are tucked in bed and dreaming with even breathing, think back over the last twenty-four hours and record a few joy-moments. Your list could include things like

- Trying a new recipe that turned out well
- A neighbor who smiled and waved
- New summer freckles on your little one's nose
- Sisters giving good-night hugs
- Brothers cheering each other on
- A forgotten piece of dark chocolate found in the back cupboard
- A friend who remembered that thing you're going through
- A short line at Walmart
- Clean pillowcases
- The first bite of peanut butter out of the jar
- A friendly cashier at the grocery store

I know I'm not the first writer to trumpet gratitude's importance. But it's a message worth touting again and again. Why? Because it's scriptural. And because it's a motherhood game changer. Every mama needs to experience the transformation that comes through intentional thanksgiving.

Finding Joy in Broccoli

I think of all the prayers I pray as a mom—prayers for safety for my kids and sanity for me. Prayers for deep sleep, strong bodies, good friends, kindness, gentleness, patience, and self-control for the whole Keife crew. None of these requests—good as they are—can trump the prayer that we would know God's will and live it out.

Knowing God's will for your life might sound lofty and complex. (I'm pretty sure it includes children eating the food they're given and mamas going to the bathroom without an audience.) First Thessalonians 5:16–18 spells it out from a different perspective: "Always be joyful. Never stop praying. Be thankful in all circumstances, for this is God's will for you who belong to Christ Jesus" (NLT). Friend, do you see it right there in black and white? Being thankful no matter what is going on in your life—in your motherhood—*is* the will of God. For you and me and the precious-crazy kids entrusted to our care. I can't see how we can become the moms God designed us to be, the moms specifically designed for our one-of-a-kind kid, apart from His will. Seems pretty clear that joy, prayer, and thanksgiving are top on the list for what it looks like to walk out our one life in cadence with God's plan.

The great news is that you can include your child in making gratitude a daily practice. Try one of these simple ways to weave thankfulness into the fabric of your day:

1. **Let your kids see you adding to your list of thanks.** Keep a journal in your diaper bag or bottomless mom-purse and jot down a blessing while you're waiting at music lessons or gymnastics practice.

2. **Give your kids an opportunity to express their gratitude.** Take time around the dinner table to ask each family member to share something they're thankful for. If your kids are super tiny, get them started by reminding them of three things that happened in the day and let them tell you which one they are most thankful for.

3. **End the day remembering the good.** Make bedtime prayers a recollection of the day's blessings. If you're too

wrung out come bedtime, practice giving thanks by re-counting joy-moments while you bathe your baby or brush your three-year-old's teeth. Even if—or rather, *especially when*—it's been a doozy of a day, you can say, "Hey, I know we've had a rough day, but let's try and remember all the good things that happened too!"

Over the last six years, giving thanks has become part of the rhythm of my life. Not that I never grumble or complain. Just ask my husband or my kids. I'm no Pollyanna, but I am a work in progress. These simple, intentional gratitude practices have made a difference. My eyes are more trained now to see the good of these days even when grinding through the hard.

My boys are slightly more grown now. This helps. Noah is ten, tall and lean and really good at most things—all strong athlete and strong will but still likes to cuddle. Elias is nine and talks nonstop; he's got a big heart (and a big dramatic streak) and loves to destroy while trying to fix things. Jude is sweet and silly at seven, a fun brother and good friend, blazing his own trail in the chaos of wild boys. As they have grown, so has my ability to choose joy in the messiness of motherhood. We may be beyond diaper explosions, teething woes, and pureed-food revolts, but each new season of motherhood ushers in its own set of challenges.

No matter what kind of day we're having or what season of motherhood we're in, we each have the ability to find the good through the lens of gratitude.

When you're up in the night holding a coughing child in a steam-filled bathroom, praying she'll stop wheezing, give thanks. When you're wiping tears from the cheeks of a boy who keeps falling off his bike and believes he'll never stay upright, give thanks. When the child you love more than life yells piercing words and slams the door in your face and you want to fall apart or rage—it's then and there that we can learn to claim the words of James: "Dear brothers and sisters, when troubles of any kind come your way, consider it an opportunity for great joy. For you know that when your faith is tested, your endurance has a chance to grow. So let it grow, for when your endurance is fully developed, you will be perfect and complete, needing nothing" (James 1:2–4 NLT).

Motherhood is an ongoing opportunity unlike any other to let our endurance grow. To let our faith take shape. Our focus is often on our child's development. Is she meeting the right milestones, putting on the right number of pounds, mastering the right skills, and adding to her vocabulary? Of course, it's part of our mama job to make sure our kids are flourishing and maturing. But growing up and into the person someone is supposed to become isn't reserved just for childhood. You've got a heavenly Father who is just as concerned about your physical health, emotional well-being, and spiritual maturity.

We know broccoli and green beans are good for our kids' bodies even if their underdeveloped palates say otherwise. We provide a variety of nutrition (gotta balance out those Chick-fil-A waffle fries and ice-cream cones!), not because we want to torture our children with something unpleasant, but because we care about their health and nutrition. God probably feels similarly as a parent, giving us a variety of experiences that will nourish us in ways sweet-and-easy, comfort-food circumstances can't.

Are we willing to open up and receive the ways God wants to grow us?

These are the days, dear mama. These are the days of squeezing joy out of chubby baby thighs and listening to the fleeting melodies of toddler lisps. These are the days of wringing gratitude out of every lighthearted moment of little-kid laughter and 1-2-3 learning. These are the days of throwing up *Help me, Jesus!* prayers when a kid gets carsick or the baby learns how to take off her diaper during nap time, then giving thanks for a washing machine that works and new mercies tomorrow. These are the days we can't afford *not* to be thankful.

Just like the glorious marathon of raising our children, the pursuit of a life rooted in gratitude will not be quick and easy.

But it will be worth it.

You Are Normal

Today a friend told me she's been losing her joy in motherhood. She remembered a talk I gave in September. "Tell me again about how we learn not to live like victims of our lives," she said. We stirred our coffee, and I saw so much of myself in this beautiful mama with three littles. How she was grappling with the beauty and strife, the love and heartache born from the same source— from the hard, gritty work of day in and day out meeting the needs of the children she bore.

I told her she was normal. I've been there too. And then I reminded her of the very best way I know to hold both the blessings and trials in surrendered hands: through the daily practice of giving thanks. Putting pen to paper for the sake of training our eyes, training our minds to see and savor and count the countless gifts we're living.

I got home and the morning rolled into afternoon and the boys came home from school and the littlest wouldn't nap and another one grumbled and the house was a mess and my throat hurt and would everyone please write their spelling words and stop asking me for another snack and for the hundredth time your feet stink so take off your socks because I can't breathe!

I excused myself from the homework fray to make a cup of tea. Light a candle. Pray. And in doing so I remembered the very words I spoke that morning that were again as much for me as for her.

I've got to keep saying it because I want to keep living it: Gratitude is the antidote for empty. Thanksgiving fills you with what is really needed—more of Jesus.

Thank You, God, for these dishes, food prepared, and bellies filled. Thank You for a morning with moms I love, a sanctuary filled with laughter and tears and twinkling lights. Thanks for grace when I yell at my kid. Tight hugs from little arms and forgiveness and chances to start again.

I cut up an apple and delivered a cup of crisp slices to each child. I walked back into the kitchen and pulled my journal out from the bottom of a wobbly stack of kid art projects and bills and printed emails that needed to be followed up on.

Pen on paper. Training my heart in thanks.

- Afternoon sun through dusty blinds
- A friend to encourage
- A house to call home
- Children
- Hope

Thank You, Jesus, for not giving up on weary mamas. Thank You for reaching into our messy days. Saving us again.

. . . .

one simple step
Choose one to practice today.

☐ Identify the internal dialogue that plays as your motherhood soundtrack. What negative thoughts or lies can you decide today to stop believing?

☐ Get a journal and write down three things you are thankful for each day this week.

☐ Spend a few minutes at the dinner table or at bedtime talking with your kids about happy moments from the day. Give thanks for the good together.

. . . .

one powerful prayer
Make this your daily prayer.

Jesus, help me to exchange complaining for thanksgiving. Give me eyes to see the good gifts You give no matter the circumstances of my day. Thank You for the joy of being a mom. Amen.

two

Stop the Crazy Making

It was a simple invitation:

Want to meet at the park by my house on
Wednesday?

That simple text triggered an onslaught of worries and what-ifs. What if the park is close to a busy street? What if the play equipment is too tall? What if Noah won't listen and Elias needs to nurse and, and, and . . .

I typed the three-letter reply before I could talk myself out of it:

YES.

Two days later I pulled into the unfamiliar parking lot, anxiety crawling up my neck. Noah wiggled out of his car seat like a toddler Houdini and was sprinting up the grassy hill before I barely lugged the stroller out of the trunk. "Stop right now!" I hollered, then strapped the baby in at lightning speed, and proceeded to huff up the hill like a dilapidated steam engine hauling cargo I wasn't fit to carry. I finally caught up with my two-year-old—praise the Lord for a broken sprinkler head that needed to be investigated. After zigzagging across the sprawling park, we eventually found my new friend, Audra, and her adorable daughter, Samantha, playing in the sandpit. *We made it!* I waved hello then doubled over to catch my breath and composure.

Audra and I had hung out a couple of times—in the next chapter I'll tell you about our first playdate where I super gracefully burst into tears in the middle of my backyard. Yeah, good times. Thankfully my breakdown didn't totally scare her away, and I was so very eager to spend more time together with the hope and prayer that our friendship could deepen into the kind of soul-sisterhood I craved. So, I plowed through my apprehensions about meeting at a foreign park and knew that whatever antics might ensue, it would be worth it for the sake of investing in a new friendship. Or so I thought.

While Audra spent the morning sitting next to Sami as she sweetly scooped sand into her bucket and shared her extra shovels with any friendly face who came near, I spent the next two hours chasing Noah around the huge outdoor complex, saving him from perilous heights, and stopping a playground flood from a random faucet my two-year-old managed to find. Audra and I barely said two sentences to each other. She was totally gracious and understanding and happily kept a watchful eye over Elias, too, as he snoozed in the stroller.

I, however, finished the playdate exhausted, fuming, and defeated. I just wanted to connect with another mom. Instead I felt like a failure and even more isolated in the challenges of raising my spirited child.

Saying yes to a new friendship is good. Extending ourselves outside our regular comfort zone or routine is good. Taking risks, trying new things, exposing our kids to new people and places and experiences—all good! But what isn't good is ignoring your gut. It isn't good to disregard what you know about how you or your child is wired for the sake of doing something you think you should be able to do.

I felt like I *should* be able to go to the park. That's a normal thing moms and kids do. It's not bungee jumping or rocket science. It's slides and swings and snacks on a picnic blanket. A playdate at a neighborhood park should be a no-brainer, right? Welp, after the twentieth time or so of a scenario that looked very similar to the one just described, I had to finally admit that, as lame as it sounds, the park was too much for us. Or we were too much for the park. However you slice it, that particular playdate destination repeatedly set me and my kid up for failure.

Noah wasn't like Sami or Cole or Kate or Lincoln or a dozen other kids we played with. Noah was Noah. Adventurous, fearless, impulsive, and a keenly selective listener. It was okay when it was just me and him. Man-to-man (or woman-to-child) defense always works best. But throw in a second, then third tiny tot with equal amounts of strong-willed gusto, and one mama manning three kids under the age of four was a match doomed for failure. There was inevitably one kid who was only content being pushed on the swing, while another child was about to fling himself onto the monkey bars his tiny arms simply could not reach, while another needed a diaper change, and on and on and on.

Now, some mothers could totally handle this situation with easy-breezy, go-with-the-flow confidence. Maybe you're that mom reading this thinking, *What's the big deal? Sounds like every day of my life. Just take it in stride!* And to you I say, Bravo! You're magnificent! Teach me all your ways because I seriously want to learn how to wrangle my children and embrace the chaos. But I also say—what I have learned to say—is that in the same way Noah is Noah, *I am me.* My child will respond to certain situations in his own unique way, and the same goes for his mama.

I was getting beat badly in the park zone—and all of us were losing because of it. But did that mean I wasn't meant to play in the motherhood game? Should I bench myself from outings with my kids for good? Of course not! I needed to identify and better understand our individual strengths and weaknesses and how we could work together as Team Keife. Forgive my love of analogies, but this was a total motherhood game changer.

A Student Mind-Set

One key to parenting with God-confidence is to become a student of your child *and* yourself. Look for emotional and behavioral patterns to determine how you both are created. Here are some questions to consider for yourself and your child:

- What energizes you?
- What makes you feel depleted?
- What fills you with joy?
- What situations trigger stress?
- What environments do you feel most comfortable in?
- What places or activities cause you to feel distracted, irritable, or overwhelmed?
- What activities or people bring out the best or worst in you?
- What situations draw you and your child closer together?
- What situations create tension, distance, or discord between you and your child?

Grab a notebook or journal and record your thoughts and observations. If you don't know the answers to these questions right off the bat, that's okay. Maybe you're so bogged down with moment-by-moment demands that you don't have the bandwidth for self-reflection. Totally fine. You don't have to produce perfect insight. I sure didn't right away—or ever. But we all have the capacity to become learners.

The next time you feel at the end of your frayed rope faster than normal, take note. The next time you get home from a playdate or party or sports practice and are seething with disappointment

42

in your child or yourself, be aware. Don't move on too quickly. Consider those icky feelings, and ask yourself:

- What's at the root of my irritation?
- Is my frustration warranted? Could it have been pre-empted by making a different decision?
- How could I help my child navigate that scenario another way?
- Does my attitude, perspective, or expectation need to change?
- What guidelines can I set that would help us better connect, behave, or respond in this kind of situation next time?

When I evaluated the whole park playdate fiasco—and how flippin' flangin' irked and sad and overwhelmed it made me feel, every time—I had to admit that that particular place was not bringing out the best in me or creating a positive bond between me and my child.

At the park, I simply wanted Noah to be a different kid. I wanted him to be a sit-and-dig-contentedly-in-the-sand kid or a go-gently-down-the-slide-a-hundred-happy-times kid, but that wasn't Noah. When I went with the added expectation that I was going to be able to have a meaningful conversation with a friend, I left no room for Noah's innate Noah-ness. Know what I mean? It wasn't reasonable for me to believe I could connect deeply with a friend *and* attend to the kid who is perpetually determined to climb a fence and sprint toward the nearest parking lot, while keeping another tiny one (or two) from choking on wood chips. Noah's personality and my expectations were setting us up for relational failure.

But here's the great news: Admitting that park playdates are not the best fit for Team Keife did not disqualify me from being a good mom! Hallelujah! The brilliance of who my boy is and the beauty of who I am as his mom did not hinge on whether or not we fared well with brightly colored jungle gyms! *Thank You, Jesus!*

On this side of the story, where unwieldy strollers and tantrums over Velcro shoes have vanished in the rearview mirror of experience, in a season where I *can* take my boy tribe to the park with friends and have a panic-attack-free good time, it's easy to see that playdates are not the litmus test of parenting success. But in the moment? In the thick of mothering three littles? It felt a whole lot different. It felt like defeat.

In reality, saying *Mercy!* to the park released me from the burning grip of self-imposed expectations. It was actually a victory!

We can't thrive as the mom God created us to be if we're trying to create a life that looks like our friends' or the ideal in our mind. We've got to take the mom we are and the child who has been entrusted to our care and make the best decisions for *that* pair.

As I took stock of our park-related feelings, reactions, and behaviors, along with the good such an activity could achieve—fresh air in our lungs, space to move squirrely bodies, an outing to break up the day, an opportunity to connect with friends—I came to the conclusion that the park was not completely off the table as a playdate option. But the boundaries for it mattered. A lot.

One crucial component of setting guidelines that will set you and your child up for success is identifying ground rules that can change the trajectory of an otherwise negative situation. Sometimes that's a mental or emotional boundary, like deliberately choosing a positive attitude, focusing on showing patience, or shifting expectations. Sometimes it's a physical boundary. Like a big ol' fence with a latching gate.

I learned I could say yes to good things while modifying the situation to make it doable, pleasant even, for me and my kids. I could say yes to a park date but save myself a lot of sweat and tears if I suggested a park that was *fully gated*. Bless all the gate builders! Now, this new rule disqualified the beautiful park near Audra and the sprawling one within walking distance of my house. But if I was willing to advocate for my preferred location and drive an extra ten to twenty minutes, the boys and I could enjoy all those park-playdate benefits while minimizing meltdowns (for them and me!).

As moms, we have to be students of our children—and ourselves. Whether your child is outgoing or shy, fearful or a daredevil, generally compliant or defiant, you don't have to stay shackled under the weight of perceived failure or inadequacy. You have the power to set boundaries and develop guidelines that will prepare you and your child for greater relational peace, connection, and growth. You can be open to advice and wisdom from others; maybe that friend on Facebook or mentor mom at MOPS will have just the solution to your particular brand of parenting challenge. But ultimately trust that *you* know your child and yourself better than anyone.

During those years with my littles, I evaluated what situations made me feel like a disaster or caused unnecessary frustration or disappointment in my kids, and I developed some new parameters. **Here's what those boundaries looked like for us:**

1. Avoid library storytime.

    We would borrow books from a friend or check them out from the library without staying for group stories. No one was forcing us to show up to the reading room at 11 a.m. on a Tuesday morning. We could happily read books we already owned for the ninety-eighth time from the comfort *of our own home!*

2. Choose only fully fenced parks.

    Not that two of my children wouldn't consistently try to climb said fence, but at least the physical barrier gave me more time to react and provided greater containment for them and peace of mind for me. Plus, in the confines of a gated park, a friend and I could actually sit and exchange more than two sentences!

3. Skip Daddy's volleyball games.

My husband is a college volleyball coach, and before we had kids, I went to all the games, knew all the players' parents, and offered my support with enthusiastic cheers. But when the boys outgrew the Bjorn, it became a stressful circus of littles who didn't understand why the bleachers weren't a jungle gym and why they couldn't chase after every ball flying through the air. Our presence was distracting to my husband and stressful for me! Why keep torturing ourselves?

4. Save grocery shopping for the weekend.

If you've ever been to Trader Joe's, you're familiar with the fresh food, healthy options, and great prices. But you also know those mini red shopping carts and super narrow aisles are hard for an autonomous adult to traverse, let alone a tired mama with three grabby kiddos who can't all fit in the cart. Just, no. We changed our routine and made grocery shopping a family affair. The extra-large carts at Costco were perfect for our kids, or I ran into TJ's alone while they stayed in the car with Dad.

These parameters weren't profound. They wouldn't have meant much to anyone else. But to me, these guidelines became a life preserver, buoying me up from my own self-condemnation and unnecessary expectations.

Finding What Works Well for You

So, what is it for you? My brand of motherhood struggle doesn't have to resemble yours in order for you to benefit from the practice of setting guidelines. Look back at those lists of questions from earlier in this chapter. What situations regularly make *you* feel like a disaster, or cause unnecessary frustration with your child or disappointment in them? Maybe you have a shy child and large birthday parties bring out the worst in both of you. You expect your kid to participate in the planned activities and happily interact with the other kids, but instead she wants to cling to your side or sit on your lap the entire time, which makes you sad or fume with "you could sit on my lap at home" frustration. Maybe large groups overwhelm your child, but he does well with one-on-one playdates.

Be mindful. Be flexible. Make necessary adjustments. Do what works well for you!

When setting boundaries, also keep in mind your strengths! This isn't just about avoiding chaos and conflict. Motherhood is a gift. Childhood is a gift. Let's live like it!

Do you get energy from being with friends? Does your child light up over opportunities to explore new places? If your daughter is in her sweet spot doing arts and crafts, think of ways to incorporate chalk and paint and glitter into your days. If your kids constantly bicker at home but find a harmonious rhythm riding bikes in the front yard or playing together at that skate park, make a mental note. Find ways to help every member of your family thrive.

It didn't take long to discover that fresh air was a special kind of soul medicine for me. This was true when I was home all day, every day with tiny kiddos, and it's still true now that my life is marked by the school-bell schedule and more hours of working and writing. For the good of my mental, emotional, physical, and spiritual health, I need to be outside for at least part of the day. Be it sunshine or a brisk breeze, palm trees or pines, there's something about connecting even a tiny bit with nature that helps me breathe deeper, slow my hurried mind, and remember the goodness of our Creator.

At the same time, I realized that my kids need a mix of indoor activities and outdoor spaces. As toddlers and preschoolers, my curious boys lit up when given the freedom to dig their fingers into dirt, fill their pockets with rocks, and touch every crunchy leaf and poke-y stick they could find. Now as growing boys on the verge of their tween years, there is still a special spark that comes when they can climb trees, run free, or build a hideout with fallen branches. There's a lot we can do in our suburban backyard, but I lean into who God made me and my kids to be when I look for ways to nourish this part of the way He designed us.

For several years in a row, our family purchased an annual pass to a nearby arboretum and botanical garden. I can't count the hours we spent weaving through the bamboo forest, counting the colors of roses in the garden, and looking for acorns with little hats as we moseyed toward the redwoods. I was often sweating pushing a double stroller along narrow paths while trying to get the boys to not splash in *every* mud puddle. These outings weren't always picturesque and more often than not included at least one meltdown by a hungry, tired, teething, or needs-to-poop child. But I never regretted the time and effort it took to make space for playing I Spy Another Butterfly and finding treasures in the form of crimson leaves and peacock feathers.

These days we take to our local hiking trails as often as we can. I'm unreasonably scared of snakes and strangers, so I only opt to go up in the foothills when my husband can lead the way and I can wander behind snapping pictures of oak trees, rays of sunshine, and the gift of my three kids.

Our outdoor adventures have changed shape over the years, and I'm sure they will continue to as our kids grow in strength and stature. But whatever form they take, being outside together has become part of the fabric of our family life. Our time in nature is a sweet intersection between what I love and need as a mama and what brings about growth and delight for my kids.

What could those intersections look like for you?

It's easy to think of setting boundaries in terms of keeping the negative stuff out. While that's definitely part of it, let's also consider the good we want to add in. How can you make space for that which is going to help you and your family thrive? How can you say yes to things that make room for your child's best qualities to flourish?

PSA of the day: Your boundaries *will* be different from your best friend's and neighbor's and those of the mom you always stand next to at school pickup. Don't compare your list of parameters to someone else's.

All the Susie Facebooks may love taking their kids to the beach every summer day, but if you have an aversion to sand and crowds and rush-hour traffic, it doesn't matter how lovely the cropped photos are of babies napping under a colorful umbrella, or toddlers collecting seashells, or teenagers playing Frisbee with wind-tousled hair. You do *you*! If your kid is going to get fried in the sun or have a tantrum over getting tangled in seaweed or dash into the waves while you're nursing a baby, then the beach will create more needless stress than blissful summer memories. Take it from me.

When my kids were all little, the moms' group I was involved with did a yearly outing to the Sawdust Factory, a woodcraft and painting place that turned your child's handprint or footprint into a creative keepsake à la Christmas ornaments and garden signs. It was one of the most popular events of the year—and I never went. Not because the paint-splattered creations weren't adorable or because I didn't want to be crafty with my kids, but because I knew myself and my boys well enough by that time to know that a multi-hour project that required sitting in one spot with access to messy acrylics was pretty much cruisin' for a bruisin', as my dad used to say. I couldn't compare where I was in motherhood with three rambunctious boys four and under with another mom who had one even-tempered child or two artsy, attentive girls. So when I let the Sawdust Factory sign-up sheet pass me by at a Thursday morning meeting, I had nothing to feel ashamed of. I was making the right call for the wiring of my particular crew.

You have nothing to be ashamed of when you say no to good things because it's the right choice for you and your child.

Hope in the Changing Seasons

Be mindful of this, mama: These self-imposed guidelines are there to empower you, not to imprison you. Whatever guidelines you come up with to best serve you and your child are intended to give you freedom! Freedom to know that you've already decided in advance to eliminate, limit, or modify the situations that bring out your worst. That is a gift. Not a punishment.

Remember this too: These guidelines are for a season. Whatever you decide will work best for your family today doesn't mean it always has to stay that way. Make changes as often as you see fit.

Now that my boys are older, our favorite park to visit is one without a fence in sight. It has a looping path perfect for bikes and scooters—classic childhood toys that for the longest time screamed, "Daredevil danger! Not suitable for children who lack spatial awareness, discernment, and impulse control." It's still altogether possible that one of our outings will lead to a collision or concussion. But my little tribe is growing in both stature and responsibility. They can whiz around the park in childhood delight while I perch under the wood pergola nursing nothing but an iced coffee. Elias with cheeks blazing pink as he powers his Razor with lightning speed. Jude grinning wide with the rickety comfort of training wheels on his lime-green minibike. Noah taking pit stops at the basketball court to shoot a layup.

Each season will have its own variety of blessings and challenges. We've got to stop fighting against the season we're in and embrace it. Embrace who you are, quirks and limitations and preferences combined. Embrace who your child is, gifts and struggles and peculiarities intertwined. Celebrate whatever childhood age and motherhood season you find yourself in.

Because here's the thing you need to really know, friend. The thing that will keep your perseverance fresh and your perspective in check: God delights in you exactly as you are, exactly where you're at. Did you know that? Do you believe it?

You don't have to have answers to all the questions I've posed in this chapter. You don't have to know what new parameters will help ease the issues with your anxious son or socially awkward daughter. You don't have to implement a new routine today nourish every sensitive, artistic, outgoing, or athletic bent your child has. You don't have to close this book and create a bullet list overnight of new boundaries with a ten-step plan to greater motherhood success. There's no pressure here. Only love and encouragement and a mama in California wildly cheering for you!

I do hope you take away some practical tips or a new framework that will help you understand yourself and your child better. I pray these tools will lead to greater freedom in your soul, peace in your home, and joy in the daily grind of life.

A Tender Heart

Even more than that, I hope you move forward knowing God is your greatest parenting partner and motherhood guide. When I was fuming and defeated at the park, God was with me. When I spoke harshly to myself, He was tender toward me. The shame and guilt heavy upon my shoulders in that season was heaped on—by me. God was there to take that unbearable load away.

You know what God was whispering to my heart through it all?

I am here with you, Becky. I see you.

You don't have to fix Noah or fix yourself. Just lean into Me. Let Me lead you into a place with more freedom and less striving. Let Me help you see that you're exactly the mom your kids need and your confidence will come from Me.

God is not trying to put you and your kids in a padded box, crossing His fingers that you mess up less. No! God is proud of the way He made you. His delight over us is what compels Him to lead, guide, teach, and refine us. "He brought me out into a spacious place; he rescued me because he delighted in me" (2 Samuel 22:20).

51

There are many times as a mom that I have cried out for rescue. Times I felt trapped inside myself or my life (wait for my chapter on mommy anger).

Sometimes stepping into the spacious place in motherhood means rooting out sin or changing a bad habit; but sometimes God rescues us and ushers us into a life-giving, soul-breathing place by helping us see ourselves the way He sees us.

What would it look like if we could delight in our own unique makeup? To be able to say with full confidence, "I praise you because I am fearfully and wonderfully made; your works are wonderful, I know that full well" (Psalm 139:14).

Let's look at ourselves and our kids with more tenderness. Let's see the good in how we're made and mother in ways that celebrate our gifts and our kids.

It wasn't just latching a park gate and steering clear of library storytime that ushered in a reprieve from my external chaos and inner turmoil. It was accepting that neither my imperfect attitude nor circumstances beyond my control could change the way God felt about me. Nothing—however good or bad or embarrassing— could change the fact that God had specifically chosen me as the one my kids call mom.

Often in motherhood there isn't much that feels sure, reliable, steady. Things with our kids are always changing. Just when you think you've conquered sleep training, your nighttime angel comes down with a cold or starts cutting a new tooth, and your restful nights become eight more excruciating hours in the motherhood marathon. Or you're sure your toddler has gotten over her separation anxiety, only to have a full-blown tantrum after months of successful Sunday school drop-offs. Or you think your third-grader has turned the corner in his math battle, only to get another disheartening progress report. Or you finally made a breakthrough with your teen and felt like you were on the same curfew/friends /communication page, only to discover he snuck out after midnight to meet up with that bad-news group. The possible scenarios that

When you're inconsistent or overlook something that was actually important, when you under-prepare or overreact, God *loves you* no more and no less.

could rock our parenting boat are endless. And often unavoidable. Sometimes stormy swells will come out of nowhere and flood our peaceful deck, choking us with the unexpected, salty foam of disappointment, discouragement, or defeat.

It's in the midst of such circumstances that I find comfort and stability in the assurance of God's steadfast love. "For I am convinced that neither death nor life, neither angels nor demons, neither the present nor the future, nor any powers, neither height nor depth, nor anything else in all creation, will be able to separate us from the love of God that is in Christ Jesus our Lord" (Romans 8:38–39).

This passage may be super familiar to you. Don't gloss over it. Read it again.

I'm pretty sure that if death and demons can't put a wedge between God's love and me, then I can trust that my quick-fire temper and my kid's willful disobedience can't either.

Nothing can build a wall between you and God's love. Nothing can disqualify you from receiving it. Not your son's finicky temperament or your daughter's wild expressiveness. Not your fatigue or embarrassment as a result of the craziness. When you make the wrong call, go to battle with your kid over something that doesn't really matter, when you're inconsistent or overlook something that was actually important, when you under-prepare or overreact, God loves you no more and no less.

In other words, the world's forces, our kid's choices, and our own crud cannot sever us from God's love.

Yesterday, today, and tomorrow. To the moon and back. He loves you. That's a boundary we can always be secure in.

. . . .

one simple step

Choose one to practice today.

☐ What situation repeatedly causes stress or frustration for you or your child? Determine one new boundary to try that could set you up for better success.

☐ What do you enjoy doing as a family? Make a list of small activities that bring you joy. Make a plan to do one this week.

☐ Grab a journal or sticky note and write out the words of Psalm 139:14: "I praise you because I am fearfully and wonderfully made; your works are wonderful, I know that full well." Thank God this week for how He has wired you and your child.

. . . .

one powerful prayer

Make this your daily prayer.

Jesus, help me to understand the unique ways You wired me and my child. Guide us into a season of greater peace, joy, and freedom in our family. Thank You for loving me no matter how I feel about my mothering. Amen.

three

I Just Want One Real Friend

We moved to our current city, nestled in the San Gabriel Valley foothills of Southern California, when Noah was six months old. It wasn't far from our first home as a married couple, just twenty freeway miles away. But it could have been a whole new state for how out of place I felt. It wasn't so much our disheveled living room and half-unpacked boxes. It had more to do with the disheveled state of my soul—overstuffed and dusty from the life-move into motherhood.

When my boy was born, I quit my job as an editor in higher-education marketing to stay home. Boy, did I love that job. I loved the people I worked with and the mix of creative collaboration and drive for individual excellence. Loved the affirmation that came from a job well done. And I loved the camaraderie of working on a team toward a greater purpose. Deciding to leave that position still meant I needed a job; living on a single income in pricey SoCal wasn't a transition we were able to make. So a month after Noah arrived, I started working part-time from home doing medical billing. (I love how God can redeem anything. The temp-job-turned-unintentional-mini-career that I never really wanted? It gave me a skill set and source of provision that I'd need years later.) For twenty hours a week, quilted together in thirty-minute blocks of time while Noah catnapped or chewed on plastic toys in the Pack 'n Play or banged around Cheerios on his high chair tray, I would tap away on my laptop. Charges in. Payments applied. Tap tap tap.

Life was full. I had a baby ninja crawling all over the house, more work than could comfortably fit in the cracks of my day, a loving husband, old coworkers who were still friends, and family within driving distance. Add in an unworldly amount of laundry from one very spit-uppy, blowouty baby, and I had more than enough to fill my time. My days as a new work-from-home mama were maxed out.

I was hardly ever by myself. Yet, I felt very, very alone. In my rookie-mama skin, this seemed too strange—too wrong—to admit. I mean, Noah was my constant shadow. We were always together, which I chose and loved. But there was no privacy or personal space in motherhood. My body was my baby's nourishment, comfort, and jungle gym.

I wasn't physically alone. But I was desperately lonely.

The woman I once was—confident, capable, a vital member of a professional team—now felt as empty as the pretty slacks and blazers that hung lifelessly in my closet. I didn't recognize the girl in the mirror anymore. And not just because of the dark circles that were now a permanent fixture below my eyes or the spit-up stained T-shirt that only slightly camouflaged my thick-strapped nursing bra. I strained to recognize the woman in the mirror because she held little resemblance to the Becky I used to be. The me who could work forty hours a week and still have energy to go to Bible study, drive an hour to meet best friends for coffee, and binge on DVD marathons of *Lost* and *24* with my husband. (Yes, this was before the wonders of streaming TV.) That girl was gone. Or at least in deep hibernation. In her place was a lost and lumpy version who loved her child and wouldn't ask to trade her life, but could barely process a complete load of laundry and make the same dry chicken tacos before collapsing into bed feeling like she worked every moment of the day and had nothing to show for it.

I felt trapped inside myself.

A decade later I can admit these feelings with ease. No matter what your "before" life looked like, your reality after becoming a mom is surely a different picture. While some women seem to slide into the role with the same beauty and grace as a Hallmark-movie birth scene—no mess or pain, all fresh-cotton-swaddle glory—I've talked to enough women to know that *every* mom, in some way or another, feels rocked by the seismic shift from not-a-mom to Mom.

I share this peek into my past freely because I want you to know deep in your bones that you are not alone. You don't have to hide your hurt or pretend you're fine. If you don't have anyone in your life who gets it—who understands the beautiful, lonely, lost, joyous tension of motherhood—know that I do. These pages are a safe place for you to sob or smile, a safe place for you to shake your head "not so much" or nod "me too."

But in my early motherhood days? Admitting that I was lonely and discouraged and a hundred other feelings I couldn't exactly name didn't feel like an option. I didn't have the words, or anyone who I thought might really understand. So I stuffed down the nagging feeling that I wasn't cut out for this mom job and kept loving my baby and doing life largely within the confines of our blue two-bedroom rental house and fenced backyard.

When I did venture out beyond our four walls, I was on a mission to find at least one mom friend. Pushing Noah on the swing at the park, wandering aimlessly at Target with a cart full of things not on my list, at the pediatrician's office—there you could find me trying to look semi put-together and pleasant, normal and approachable while sopping up baby drool. You know, as if to say, "Come talk to me. I'm not awkward. I'm good friend material."

My eyes well with tears for that floundering mom I used to be. For that Becky who yearned for meaningful friendships but didn't know how to cultivate them in a new town with one, then two, then three little boys in tow. For that precious mama who just needed to know she wasn't alone.

The Flip Side of Loneliness

What I didn't realize then but I know with my whole heart now is that even in that lonely, aching season of life, I wasn't actually alone. There was a Friend always waiting for me. I just wasn't aware that He was there.

I could weep for the ways God has filled my aching with His presence and abundantly answered my prayers with incredible, life-together friends. I'm overwhelmed with gratitude for how God has worked through my story and how fiercely I want you to see Him in your story too.

I want you to live in the kind of freedom where you can cry out to God, tell Him all your fears and desires, and know that He hears, He cares, and He is working on your behalf. If you're in a pit of loneliness where doubts about yourself and motherhood are your closest companion, I want to see you journey into a place of confidence in community. I want you to grab hold of the assurance that God did not make a mistake in making you the mom of your kids and that He will provide what you need to thrive. I want to link arms and believe together that He will lavish us with everything from wisdom and energy to one or two (or ten) share-the-joys-and-burdens-of-motherhood-with friends.

I cling to this promise for you and for me: "Being confident of this, that he who began a good work in you will carry it on to completion until the day of Christ Jesus" (Philippians 1:6).

As moms, we can know without a doubt that God has begun a good work in us—He entrusted us with children! Now it's our turn to trust Him. Trust Him with yourself. Trust Him with your baby or big kid. Trust Him with your full schedule and empty friendships. Trust Him with your longings and insecurities. Go ahead and take every nook and cranny, shiny and grimy aspect of your life—you can trust God with it all.

Here's why God is trustworthy: He goes with us.

God does not open a door, push us through, and yell, "Good luck!" then slam it behind us and wipe His hands on His heavenly robes in a *good riddance, that's done* kind of way. No way! If God knit a child in your womb or gave you the gift of adopting a son or daughter (a profound reflection of our adoption into the family of God), then He is committed to seeing this motherhood plan through with you.

At the core of my loneliness as a mom was feeling alone in my circumstances and unknown in my struggles. But guess what? While those feelings were real and God cared enough to help me move into a place of cultivating the kind of life-together friendships I longed for, in reality I was neither alone nor unknown. God was always with me. He never once left me. And He knew me intimately.

In Psalm 139, David unpacks this beautiful truth:

> You have searched me, LORD,
> and you know me.
> You know when I sit and when I rise;
> you perceive my thoughts from afar.
> You discern my going out and my lying down;
> you are familiar with all my ways.
> Before a word is on my tongue
> you, LORD, know it completely.
> You hem me in behind and before,
> and you lay your hand upon me.
> Such knowledge is too wonderful for me,
> too lofty for me to attain. (Psalm 139:1–6)

In heaven and on earth, in sorrow and despair, in great blessing and great delight, in every place and every season, you are not alone. God does not leave you. I love how a few verses later David points out how God's knowledge of him has been intimate and complete since the beginning: "For you created my inmost being; you knit me together in my mother's womb" (Psalm 139:13).

Friend, God knew you before you took your first breath and He knows you now. Take a deep breath. Sit with that for a minute.

As I look back on my years of motherhood—the hard and the holy, the miraculous and the mundane—I'm grateful for the profound ways God has grown me through it all. Second only to Scripture, the thing God has used to encourage me and minister to me in the thick of motherhood more than anything else is friendships. Intentional friendships. Hands down.

But how did I go from that lonely mom to one thriving in friendship? I made mistakes and I learned from them.

I stopped relying only on myself, stopped feeling sorry for myself, and let God lead me. This meant letting other people into my mess and being willing step into theirs. Was it always easy? No. But it was worth it.

It is still worth it. Let me tell you the story.

I've always believed friendships are important. As soon as I became a mom, I knew that I should probably start building my "mom tribe"—heaven knows I couldn't figure out this mama life on my own. I had heard of a gathering of moms at local churches called MOPS (Mothers of Preschoolers), so I went on their website and found a group that met near my home. When Noah was just a month old, we started attending. I was grateful for something to look forward to every other Friday morning. I enjoyed the yummy breakfast I didn't have to cook, the lovely speakers, and the nice women I sat with around my assigned table. But this biweekly engagement with other moms wasn't a pretty bow on my friendship story. At the end of that spring semester, I didn't feel any more known than when I first began. I had spent two and a half hours every other week politely chitchatting and awkwardly nursing my son in public, but I didn't build meaningful friendships.

That summer was when we moved to be closer to my husband's job, and I repeated the same steps. Found a moms group at a local church. Enjoyed the twice-a-month interaction with other adults while sweet nursery workers played with my teething baby. Everything was pleasant. But it stayed on the surface. I still didn't have another mom to call *friend*.

I quickly got pregnant with baby number two. When Elias was born, my joy doubled, but so did my loneliness. I felt isolated. Stuck in my house, chained to the rhythms and routines of a feisty toddler and new baby. I was aching in my motherhood skin without a single friend to call during the day. Not one mama to text to meet for a walk or playdate at the park. Not one fellow professional diaper-changer or bottle-warmer who understood the privilege and pain of motherhood. I didn't have a close confidant who understood the ins and outs of peekaboo and jammie snuggles or the woes of stain-removing and hands chapped from dishwashing. Sometimes a girl just needs to know there is someone else living through the sleep-deprived struggles and glorious joys of the mom job too.

I loved my children deeply. Man, did I love them—*do* I love them! But that all-consuming love was consuming me. It wasn't a physical loneliness. God knows I was desperate for a moment alone! *Why is a mother seated on the porcelain throne a magnet for a child's most urgent needs and inquiries?* I was physically surrounded by my children, but my loneliness wouldn't lift. I had joined a moms group. Mingled hopefully at the park and children's bookstore surrounded by other tots and mamas. What else was I supposed to do?

It was at this point that I did what I should have done from motherhood day one: I prayed specifically. I prayed intentionally. I told God how I felt like I was flailing and failing and I didn't know if it would ever change. I asked Him for one life-together friend who could help me find my way up and through motherhood.

One weekend when Elias was two months old, which made Noah a mere twenty-one months, I threw my back out. Chris was out of town. I could barely move. I couldn't bend over to get Noah out of his crib or lift Elias out of the bassinet. In a panic, I called my nearest relative, my Aunt Diann. She came to my rescue, armed with a heating pad, Bengay, and patience to help wrangle a rambunctious toddler. We got the baby fed and Noah doing something within the confines of relative safety. (Did I mention that at this stage Noah could hardly talk but he could climb to great heights and launch his body into the air like a flying squirrel?) Then Diann instructed me to lie down so she could try to massage out the spasmic knots in my back.

She rubbed and I cringed. I tried to remember that sometimes pain is productive. Sometimes you have to go through the working out of what's knotting you up in order to come into healing and relief. As Diann pushed and pressed, she asked how I was doing as mama of two littles. She asked if Chris and I had found a home church yet, if I had made any mama friends. Between breathe-through-the-pain gasps, I explained how we hadn't settled on a church since we'd moved, and I had tried these moms groups but they felt fruitless in the friend-making department, so I didn't think I would go back.

Lord, please heal my back.

"I've told you about Mom to Mom, right?" she asked.

"No, I don't think so."

My aunt went on to describe a warm and friendly, deeply authentic group of moms of all ages at her church, which was just one quick suburban city over. "You should really check it out!" she said. "You will love it."

I've already tried this, I thought.

Elias started to fuss in his bouncy seat, and I hadn't seen Noah in too many quiet minutes. "Can you check on the boys?" I asked.

As I lay there on my living room rug, irritated by the crumbs pressing into my skin and unable to recall the last time I ran the vacuum, my spirit cried out in gratitude for my aunt's help. I couldn't have gotten through the day without her. *Thank You, Lord, for helping me in my time of need.*

I sensed God reply in my spirit, *I will always help you in your time of need. But you have to be willing to keep walking through the doors I open for you.*

Recognize Friendship Pitfalls

Three weeks later, my back was still giving me some issues, but it was strong enough for me to get dressed, load two kids in the car, and drive to a new moms group. This was my third time walking into an unfamiliar church, into a crowded room of women where I knew no one. In a way it felt like setting myself up for disappointment déjà vu.

But a couple things were different this time: I was boldly clinging to my prayers for one in-the-thick-of-it mama friend. I believed that God would meet my need through this open door. I also had a resolution in my heart that I know was from the Lord because it's not an idea I conjured up on my own: *Be the friend you long to have.*

I had to identity what wasn't working about my friendship pursuits up to that point and take responsibility for my part. In the process, I recognized several pitfalls that caused my previous attempts to fail before they even got started, or kept them on the surface even when I longed to go deeper.

See if any of these pitfalls ring true for you.

1. False Thinking
    "I'm new, so others should come to me." It's the number one new-girl culprit of staying in the lonely zone. In those first two mom groups, I assumed it was up to others to

seek me out, to take the conversation deeper, to initiate additional hangouts. I put the responsibility on everyone else—so when friendships didn't pan out, I felt like a powerless victim. False! New or old, introvert or extrovert, we each have to take ownership of our own friendships. If you want to get to know other moms in a deeper way, be the one to go deeper. If you're new to a group, don't wait for others to notice you. Plan with purpose and courage to be the friend you long to have.

False thinking also says, "Everyone else already has their friend plate full." It's easy to walk into a moms group, women's Bible study, yoga class, or PTA meeting and think that everyone there already has three best friends and a large group of close companions. It's easy to assume there are cliques and in-crowds and they're all too full so you're automatically relegated to the outside. While that might be partially true in some circumstances—and I'm sad if that's been a reality you've experienced—I also know this: I have yet to meet a woman who doesn't long for deeper friendships.

Over years of writing and speaking to thousands of women, I have heard a universal longing for intimate, authentic friendships. We have a great capacity for love and connection. Don't presume you know what's in another woman's heart. There's a good chance you are exactly the kind of friend she's longing for too.

2. Snap Judgments

It's embarrassing to admit, but I've been guilty of making snap judgments about people, which then color my perceptions of them and my openness to deeper connection. The truth is, our first impressions often don't pan out. A few months into my new moms group, I remember someone asking me how it was going. "All the moms at my table are nice," I said, "but I just don't think I'll really click with anyone." Oh, what a slow learner I am.

One of those moms was Desiree, who is one of my dearest friends, eight years and counting. Hold your first impressions loosely. Give yourself time (lots of time!) before deciding whether you have a kindred connection with a potential new friend. Sometimes the very best layers aren't the most easily visible. We lose out big time when we jump to conclusions about someone's personality or character.

3. Insecurity

"I'm too _____" [fill in the blank]. I'm too shy, too loud, too broken, too emotional, too socially awkward, messy, self-conscious, weird. We all have our thing that feels like it's going to be too much (or not enough) for someone else. Rarely do our insecurities rear their ugly heads like they do in the presence of other women we don't know well. Heap on the added pressures of motherhood—*Will she judge the way I dress, feed, discipline, or sleep train my kid?*—and you've got a gaping hole of what-ifs waiting to consume the possibility of meaningful friendship.

How do we avoid falling into this insecurity pit? Remember this: God made you YOU! Your shyness and weirdness are part of what makes you beautifully you. Plus, we are all a work in progress. I'm a totally awkward phone talker, and when I get really excited, I stutter. And sometimes I try to be funny and it comes out as lame or insensitive. I could let these quirks and flaws build a wall between myself and others. Or I can admit, yep, I'm not perfect! But I still need friends, and I still have a lot of qualities that make me a good one.

Bottom line: Friendship was God's idea! God himself exists in community—the Trinity, the triune God, three in one—a lived-out expression of God's relational nature. We each embody this relational wiring as children made in His image. There's no way He is going to leave you out! He has life-together friends for all of us.

But what if I try to be her friend and she doesn't like me? (Or maybe I don't really like her?), you might whisper to yourself. I know I have. True, not every mom will be your next BFF or a kindred-spirit connection. But doesn't every woman have value? Can't we learn something from everybody? Even if a friendship attempt doesn't pan out, you can still be a bright spot in another mama's day, or at the very least give thanks for a shared cup of coffee.

Don't let insecurities or what-ifs steal your chance at deep friendships.

4. Good Intentions with No Follow-Through

This is probably the biggest cause of failed friendships. You *feel* like you're trying hard to put yourself out there, to push past the surface and grow authentic friendships. But too often we spend a whole lot of mental energy in the arena of good intentions but don't actually demonstrate active follow-through. The classic example? "We should hang out sometime!" I know you've said it. So have I!

You meet a new mom at church or preschool, or your husband introduces you to his colleague's wife and you think you could hit it off. The words roll off your tongue smooth and easy, "We should hang out sometime." She likely says, "Oh, I'd love that," and you both nod in pleasant agreement. And then . . . nothing. You don't exchange numbers. You don't call or text her. You don't make a plan. And that good intention falls to the wayside of inaction. I don't know any two women who ever became soul sisters simply because they *thought* it would be a good idea to get together.

No matter what season of motherhood you're in—babies and toddlers or hormonal junior-highers—we all need friends to journey with, women who stand with us and are for us. Not one of us is better alone. *Together* is where we thrive!

Inviting Others

So how do we move away from these pitfalls and toward healthy friend-building that really works? If we want to build intentional friendships, the first thing we have to do is be willing to *initiate*.

If you're going to utter those perfectly polite, well-meaning words, "We should hang out sometime," decide ahead of time that you're going to follow through. You've got to initiate. If you're already shaking your head in no-can-do or I've-already-tried-that refute, let me tell you, *You can do this, and it is worth it.* If you're an extreme introvert or you've been stung by the brutal bee of friendship rejection too many times and you're feeling can't-put-myself-out-there-again shy, please don't break out in hives. You were made for this.

Here's what I've learned needs to happen when you initiate:

First, you need to make it timely (i.e., follow up right away). When too many days or weeks go by between chatting with that mom at storytime or introducing yourself during the (awkward) meet-and-greet at church and following up, you just won't do it. I'm speaking from experience. We get all weird. *Will she remember me? Did she really want to hang out? It's been two weeks—I can't text her now.* Avoid all the hemming and hawing and make a plan as soon as you say you'd like to get together.

When you do follow up, make it manageable. For me, this was the main reason my good intentions fell flat. As much as I wanted close friends—really, any friends—actually spending time with other moms and their kids in the midst of my already chaotic life felt very overwhelming. I had to learn to make time with friends manageable.

Not one of us
is better alone.
Together is where
we *thrive!*

When my kids were little, my windows between naps and nursing were small, so I chose the best time frame that fit the rhythm of our day. I also decided not to stress out that it didn't feel like very much. This meant saying to a new friend, "Want to come over from 10 to 11:30 to play in my backyard and eat Popsicles?"

No matter what kind of sleepless night I had, no matter how cranky or compliant my kids decided to be, we could handle hanging out with people and Popsicles for ninety minutes. As my kids got older and my schedule got fuller in a different way, my go-to method of manageable initiation was to invite someone to grab coffee for an hour before school pickup. Clear start and stop times. Clear expectations about activities and locations. Figure out what speaks the language of "yeah, that's manageable" to you, and do that. Your friendship efforts don't have to be long or elaborate. Just reach out.

As you initiate in a timely, manageable way, also **be mindful to identify and remove scary barriers**. What do I mean? I mean, take the pressure off yourself! Name the friendship expectations that could be holding you back and then give yourself grace and space to do something different. Do you feel like you can't invite people over if your house isn't up to a certain standard of tidiness? Buy yourself a big bin that you can throw all the junk in fifteen minutes before someone comes over. No one has to look in your front closet or bedroom. Does the thought of hosting a large play-date send you into a frantic tizzy? Don't volunteer to have all eight moms and their nineteen kids from your moms-group table over. Let someone else host or suggest a local (gated) park.

The scary barrier I had to remove from my building-friendships equation was lunch. Oh yes, lunch can be scary! Because when you have two won't-sit-still toddlers and a food-throwing baby, it's not exactly the prime environment for a meaningful conversation. Not to mention that my lunch usually consisted of peanut butter and jelly sandwich crust and the remnants of someone's abandoned yogurt cup. Not what I could call an appetizing invitation. If I couldn't feed myself a real meal and get my kids to keep their tiny buns in their chairs, how in the world was I going to fix and serve lunch for others while managing my circus? I feel a little breathless just remembering it.

But other moms host lunch playdates! Other moms make themed bento boxes of nutritional cuteness for all the kids while whipping up a gorgeous grown-up pasta salad worthy of a restaurant menu. News flash! I don't have to be like other moms. And neither do you!

Lunch was too much for me. Therefore, in that season of raising littles, I would not plan a playdate around lunch. Boom! Scary barrier removed. And if a hangout did spill over into the noon hour? That mama friend was welcome to fix her kids a PB&J on a paper plate shoulder to shoulder with me. And for us mamas? "Cereal's in the pantry and milk's in the fridge."

Another extraordinary yet simple way to initiate with new friends or go deeper with women you already know is to **invite someone into what you're already doing**. Whether you're a full-time stay-at-home mom, a full-time work-out-of-the-house mom, or straddling both worlds as a work-from-home mom like me, your life is full. Building community will lead to a profound blessing and doesn't have to feel like a burden in the process.

Think about how you already spend your days and ask someone to step into that time with you. For me, this often meant inviting another mom to go on a walk. Walks were my sanity and saving grace when my boys were little. Noah and Elias in the double stroller, Jude strapped to my body, snacks for days, and off we went to inhale fresh air, spy on every bird, and look at all the trees.

Our local downtown area had sidewalks wide enough to fit two strollers side by side. So I'd say, "Hey, New Friend, I walk in the village most mornings around ten. Is there a day this week you'd like to join me?" This was how I made my very first mom friend, Sarah. We met at Mom to Mom and I asked her to go on a walk. Over the months of Sarah's maternity leave, we logged many miles pushing our strollers side by side, up and down our gumdrop tree-lined main street. I was so grateful to discover that part of my regular motherhood rhythm could become an opportunity for friendship connection.

What do you like to do with your kids or solo? Going to the trampoline park or splash pad? Invite another mom along. It could be the lifeline she needs to break up her own long day with littles. Longing for a pedicure or to try that new little bakery? Build into a friendship by asking someone to go with you.

My husband travels quite a bit for work, which can make having a girls' night out hard. Instead of feeling disqualified from potential evening plans with friends, I used the time I had and invited another mom over after bedtime on nights my husband was gone. I'd text a friend whom I wanted to invest in:

> Chris is out of town this week. Want to come over on Tuesday or Wednesday night at eight?

In one season, this is how my friend Kristy became one of my favorite people. She'd roll up in her sweat pants and knock ever so softly, careful not to wake the sleeping angels. We'd sit on my couch until our eyes couldn't stay open, sharing stories and laughter and tears. I poured cups of hot tea, and Kristy pulled dark chocolate out of her purse. There were still books and blocks and random socks strung about the living room. But none of that mattered when two moms got to prop up their feet together and commiserate and dream and just be seen.

What are you doing this week? Ask God to help you see spaces in your regular routine to turn into opportunities for investing in friendships. Ask God to whisper a name to your heart. A woman you'd like to get to know. Maybe someone who is secretly flailing and needs the gift of a life-together friend. God won't give you more hours in your day (trust me, I've asked!), but He will help you use what you have to meet your deepest needs.

Finally, keep reaching out! One or two playdates aren't going to translate into deeply knowing someone and being known. You have to spend time together. It doesn't always have to be a serious conversation. Trying to piece together intelligent thoughts and heartfelt words over the happy shrieking of a Chick-fil-A play place isn't always doable—but consistent time together builds a foundation for your friendship. The moments will add up.

Embracing Messy Vulnerability

As we learn to become queens of initiating, we then get to step into the beautiful, terrifying territory of *being vulnerable*.

I was getting pretty good at putting together all those pieces of the initiating puzzle. It was paying off. I was enjoying the sweet fruit of new friendships. I had a friend to text when I was itching for a playdate or needed a pediatrician recommendation. But fairly quickly I discovered that it would take more than Popsicles and walks to develop the kind of intentional, mothering shoulder-to-shoulder community I longed for.

Five months after starting Mom to Mom, my family began going to another local church. I was so thankful for my budding moms-group circle of friends, but I had a desire to grow roots at our new home church. I figured having a friend in my same season of life would be a good way to start.

One Sunday, the usher escorted Chris and I to a row on the far side of the small worship center. We sat down in the designated row next to another couple. After the songs and sermon were done, I started chitchatting with this beautifully pregnant mom, asking the usual questions: What's your name? Do you have other kids? When are you due? When I heard Audra had a daughter about Noah's age, I mustered up a quick dose of courage and asked if she'd like to get together sometime. She said yes, and then I awkwardly asked for her number and scribbled the digits on my church bulletin. (Why does making friends as an adult feel a whole lot like dating?)

I took my own advice and texted Audra a day or two later, and you can bet my invitation included backyard frozen treats. The playdate day came and Audra and her adorable daughter Sami were right on time. (Yes, this is the same lovely mama-daughter pair I mentioned in the last chapter.)

I'll save you every detail about the block towers Sami built that Noah knocked down and the shovels he refused to share and the way Elias wailed inconsolably instead of taking his regular nap. Let's fast-forward to the part where I burst into uncontrollable tears in the middle of the backyard. In front of a woman who was pretty much a stranger. Yep. *Awkward.*

In that moment, I realized I had a choice to make about what I was going to do with those tears: (a) I could make excuses. "Oh, the baby is teething and Noah was up all night. We're all exhausted. You've just caught us on a bad day." (b) I could pretend I was okay. "Oh, wow, I've got some dust in my eye and it's messing with my contacts. Will you excuse me for a second?" (c) I could ask her to leave. "I'm sorry about the crying baby and selfish toddler. We need to take a rain check. Or (d) I could take a risk and be vulnerable; I could share about the hard spot I was in on my motherhood journey. Thankfully, this is what I did.

I let Elias cry in the baby swing and I let Noah keep digging in the planter, and I stood in the middle of the grass and let the tears fall. I told this mom with the super calm spirit and sweet demeanor that I loved the gift of mothering my sons, but I also felt sad and lost. I felt like I was struggling in a role I should inherently know how to do. I told her parenthood makes marriage better and harder, and sometimes it's hard to know who I am as a wife and who we are as a couple. I told her that I was grateful for an income, but I felt like I was drowning with my part-time job . . . and how none of this was all good or all bad and there was no clear resolution or change in sight.

Audra listened sympathetically. She was kind and reassuring. I think most women are.

This was definitely not the playdate I planned for or wanted, but my untimely meltdown was actually a God-gift—the beginning of one of my most-treasured friendships.

If you let your guard down enough to let the realness leak out, it frees others to do the same.

. . . .

one simple step
Choose one to practice today.

☐ If you're in a season of loneliness, start praying for one life-together friend. Ask God to show you open doors and how to be the friend you long for.

☐ Identify an area of false thinking or insecurity that has kept you from cultivating deep friendships. Replace that lie with a truth of who God says you are. Write it down and read it every day this week.

☐ Think about the rhythms in your week and what you're already doing. Then, initiate plans with a friend in a way that feels manageable to you!

. . . .

one powerful prayer
Make this your daily prayer.

Jesus, thank You that You know me and are always with me even when I feel alone. Give me a brave heart to invest in friendships right where I am. Help me to take the necessary steps to embrace the gift of doing life together. Amen.

four

It's Okay to Need Your Village

I leaned against my kitchen sink, the one stacked with enough dirty dishes to hide the mysterious brown spots that needed to be scrubbed off, and took another deep breath. It had been a long week. A long couple of months, really. I felt so behind on ordinary life, and I only half cared because the big, hard stuff that people I loved were going through made my crusty sink and loads of wrinkled laundry seem meaningless.

My head spun with details. I was trying to manage schedules and scrounge up child care during my husband's busiest work season so I could go out of town to attend my friend's memorial service. My thirty-two-year-old, mother-of-two-little-ones, radiant friend had lost her battle with cancer. I desperately wanted to make the seven-hour drive to celebrate Alyssa's beautiful life. There were still so many pieces up in the air, but at least I had Desiree locked in to care for my littlest, Jude.

I glanced back at the dishes but picked up my phone instead. It was hard to think through the heart-swirling emotions and mind-whirling list of to-dos. But I managed to pluck out a text to Des with my departure and drop-off plans and rambled a list of thanks for all the other ways she had recently helped me. I finished the text with a confession:

> I feel like I've been a really needy friend lately, and you are always there to help so willingly. Thank you. I appreciate you beyond words and hope that at some point I can return all the favors.

Within a moment I heard the familiar bing-bong of a new message back.

> Don't be silly! Friendship is way more than favors. It's life together!! I love you dearly.

I read her words. And then read them again, slowly allowing each one to mark my heart like the fresh tears staining my cheeks.

My dear friend was so right. Friendship is way more than favors. In fact, that's something I would have said had the roles been reversed. It's my joy to help my friends! I'm thankful when I'm able to meet a tangible need for someone I care for or come alongside a friend to understand their hurts or celebrate their triumphs. But as the one who had to do the help-asking, the one whose tears flowed frequently, whose practical and emotional needs had been many, I'd fallen into a guilt trap of thinking that *I* was too much. Of believing that my friends were keeping a record of favors given and favors owed.

The temptation was to believe that as soon as life calmed down and I got my act together, I needed to start paying back all the good deeds to even the score. But the truth is, there is no score-keeping with real friends. We build community by bearing each other's burdens, and sometimes that means being willing to let yourself be the one carried.

Several days later I pulled into Desiree's driveway and unloaded my two-year-old and his backpack full of overnight gear. We walked up the terra-cotta path, and Jude stood on his tippy-toes to reach the doorbell. When Des opened the door, Jude happily joined the beautiful chaos of a home full of children. I hugged my sweet friend, comforted by the assurance that she was happy to be doing life together, which today meant serving me by loving my son.

The Soil of Service

Like we talked about in the previous chapter, initiating and being vulnerable are crucial to starting meaningful friendships. That's how I got to this scene with Desiree.

But how do seedling friendships grow deep roots and lasting fruit? In the soil of service.

The richest friendships I have are the ones where we have been intentional to serve one another and let ourselves be served. This plays out both in times of crisis and in the everyday mundane.

The January after I started going to Mom to Mom, my dad suddenly passed away. I had a two-year-old and a six-month-old, and I felt swallowed by the mingle of daily life and crashing grief. In those blurry first weeks of crushing sorrow, planning my dad's funeral, and dealing with all of his possessions, I didn't know what I needed. A text came from a mom I hardly knew:

We'd like to bring your family some meals.

When I didn't know how to ask for help, new friends gave the gift of showing up. They came with big bowls of pasta and cheesy chicken casserole. I opened the door to my messy house and splotchy red cry-face and received their hugs and dishes wrapped in aluminum foil. My saying yes and their willingness to come was like a hard, achy, beautiful tilling of soil, preparing the way for deeper friendships to grow.

One of my first mom friends in that season also showed me what it looked like to share the weight of our everyday burdens. I once told Amy about how I was dreading taking one of the boys for his annual checkup. Every time we went to the pediatrician, we were like a three-ring circus barging into that quiet office. Between the kid who wouldn't sit still to get his ears checked and another one overly curious about the hazardous waste container and a third acting like he'd been deprived of food and sleep for a week, this flailing ringleader couldn't get through the show without sweating through my shirt and fighting back tears.

Now, another appointment was four days away, and I already felt the proverbial hives burning under my skin.

"Just take the kid who needs to go and drop the other two off with me," Amy said.

"Umm, really? Are you sure?"

"Of course."

It hadn't even crossed my mind to ask for help. I just considered every doctor's office meltdown part of my motherhood duty that must be endured on my own. Amy helped me see that her temporary inconvenience of having two extra kids to look after was worth it for the gift it gave me—less public-parenting stress and more focused attention for one kid. I was so grateful.

Because of Amy's example, I started looking for ways to give a similar gift. Like offering to watch a friend's kids so she can get her hair cut *alone*. No one can relax when they have a toddler rolling in fallen hair scraps or turning a salon chair into a whirling rocket of doom. Giving ninety minutes to free up another mama for something she wants or needs is a simple way to strengthen the bonds of friendship.

We've all heard the saying "It takes a village a raise a child." Well, guess what? It's okay to need your village! It's okay to not be able to do it all on your own. I have experienced God's tender love and extravagant care through bags of groceries and free babysitting, through loaned cars and chicken soup. It's not only okay to need your village, it's part of God's very best plan for you. It's His way of reminding you day in and day out that He sees you.

We build a village by reaching out to others in their time of need and inviting others to step into our daily struggles and hardest trials.

Over the years my village has shifted and changed. Yours won't always look the same in every season either. But a community is always needed. After several years with Mom to Mom, God led me to leave that group and help grow a ministry for moms at my home church. It's been six years, and this community of women has loved me and taught me what friendship really looks like.

The thing about serving one another is that it's contagious. Serving in community multiplies our efforts and our joy. The more we love in word and action and on our knees in prayer, the more God empowers us to keep on loving.

As moms, we pour out everything we've got for our children, so much so that it can feel like there's nothing left to give. I have lived that feeling—a lot. It's counterintuitive to think that giving more of ourselves could actually be the way of being filled back up. But it's true. If you've never experienced this, if you're stuck in a place of only feeling wrung out, trust me: God really can supply for your needs as you help meet the needs of others. I've seen it over and over and over again. My word, it's beautiful.

Sending Out an SOS

The moms ministry team I'm a part of has a group-text chat. Early in the morning and late at night, in the five o'clock witching hour and the in-between moments, texts come through asking for prayer. The requests range from the normal grind to heart-aching trials: stomach flu, leaky pipes, toddler tantrum, gotta find a new house, going into labor, starting another round of chemo. These women rally with Target runs and coffee drop-offs and extravagant "love bombs." A basket of cozy socks, snacks, and books might just be what a friend sitting next to her child's hospital bed needs to get through another day of the impossible.

It only takes each person giving a little to make a big impact.

I've preached the "it's okay to need your village" message to myself on repeat. On weeks I feel like I should be able to keep a hundred balls in perfect orbit, only to watch them come crashing down, leaving goose-egg welts on my head and pride, I'm not above saying the words out loud: *It's okay to need your village, Becky.*

I recently sent an SOS text to friends, confessing that Chris is traveling and fevers are raging and my anxiety is rising because I can't quit motherhood or work or grad school. When you're mothering solo, there's no quarantining yourself in bed for Netflix-watching solitary confinement. (You single mamas and military mamas are ROCK STARS in my book.)

Yet even after I reached out to my tribe, I still battled my internal dialogue: *I chose to be a mom, and I'm grateful for my husband's job, and I signed up for grad school, and other people would long for the kind of work I get to do. I shouldn't need help or complain. What woman hasn't pulled herself up by her feverish bootstraps and cleaned up puke?*

Not one friend replied with, "Suck it up, Becky, you brought this on yourself." No! One friend went to the pharmacy for me and another dropped off a bag full of coloring books, echinacea tea, and Kleenex without being asked. Not with judgment or out of obligation, but because when we see our friends hurting, it's a gift to help be the bringers of a little relief.

Admitting your needs and saying *yes* to help is not easy for most of us! But your yes not only blesses you, but it will bless the friend who wants to help.

That's how my friendship with Sara really started to grow deep roots. We had a mutual "liking" of one another. You know, that feeling. *She seems great. I'd enjoy getting to know her more, but I'm not sure if it will happen.* But our friendship deepened rather quickly because she was quick to offer tangible support (and I was quick to accept it).

My mind scrolls back through all the friendship years spent in the soil of service. One particular day stands like a garden stake, marking a season of blessing and growth. Five years flash by. The moment feels like yesterday. . . .

I pulled my hands from the water and wiped the suds straight on my jeans. I crouched down to see eye to eye with my four-year-old, breathe deep, and listen to his most urgent cry:

"Mommy, my brudders are not being kind and caring for me at all! They aren't playing with me or helping me fight the lava monsters! And that is RUDE!!"

We talked *again* about using our words and how sometimes we need to join what someone else is doing or play alone. Elias wiped his runny nose along his sleeve and dinosaur-stomped back to his room, big tears holding fast in the corners of his eyes. I turned back to the dishes and let my gaze rest on the mason jar filled with sunflowers sitting on the windowsill. Deep-yellow petals encircled mocha centers like golden crowns. Blooms of sunshine resting on sturdy, green stems. Flowers from a friend.

I understood how my middle boy felt. He wants to be *with*. He longs to be seen. Known. Valued and included. I get it.

Suddenly my own fat tears appeared. Not because I was distressed about Elias. But because I was newly impressed with the deep soul blessings God had poured out on me through friends. I have known the ache of emptiness. The deep pain of loneliness. And I know the joy of being filled. These happy blossoms catching afternoon light were just one of many beautiful gifts born from the seed of friendship.

I think again about Monday morning and what started with a simple *How was your weekend?* text from a friend. I shared the highlight of a nature scavenger hunt and gratitude for Chris returning from a work trip. I almost left it at that. But I chose to be fully real and reveal that the weekend in fact didn't end so great. My two-year-old woke up in the night with a sudden onset of croup. He was unable to breathe, and I rushed him to the ER, where we spent an unpleasant four hours.

> We didn't get home till after 3 a.m., so now I
> feel like Zombie Mommy. But thankfully Jude
> is doing much better and I'm hopeful for the
> chance of an afternoon nap.

Without skipping a beat, Sara replied back.

> Oh, no!!! Can I bring you dinner?

Now I faced another decision: decline help because I could handle the day on my own or accept dinner and be tangibly blessed while deepening our friendship. The leftover refried beans in the fridge flashed in my mind, and I reasoned how I could ask my husband to pick up tortillas and we'd be fine for dinner. Yes, I would be fine without help. But what if being *fine* isn't the point?

I accepted Sara's gracious offer, and a few hours later I heard a soft knock. I opened the door to arms full of delicious delights: shredded barbecue chicken with soft rolls for sandwiches, tender-crisp green beans, sliced strawberries, olive oil chips, and Caesar salad. A little "Get Well" balloon peeked through the spectacular smorgasbord. I grew giddy when I spied a box of Magnum mini ice-cream bars, because apparently Zombie Mommies need dark chocolate to survive. Oh, yes.

I thanked my friend profusely. The light in her eyes beamed a genuine pleasure for the opportunity to help.

The next day Sara sent a follow-up text to see how my little guy was feeling and asked if I needed anything from the store. Again, I hemmed and hawed in my mind—*we could get by for a few more days without milk and bananas; I really didn't want to put her out.* But, again, the deeper truth about my situation rang clear in my heart: I need deep friendships.

On my journey from isolation in a new city and new life stage to thriving in a community of do-life-with friends, I have learned over and over that meaningful friendships are forged in the soil of

84

We are meant to come *alongside.* To lean in and be held up. To do the *holding.*

service. We are meant to come alongside. To lean in and be held up. To do the holding.

Later, Sara arrived with the items I asked for . . . and a bouquet of sunflowers.

Service helps foster trust and loyalty in relationships. It's an investment in each other's lives. It's living the great commandment to love one another. Now, I have certainly missed opportunities to build some friendships by saying no to help that was offered or by not embracing a chance to serve when I could have. I'm sure it goes without saying, but don't get hung up on trying to help your friends perfectly or expect someone to swoop in to your rescue every time something in life goes awry. This isn't about being each other's savior. There is only One of those. Yet, we experience more of Christ when we lean into the call to love.

One of my favorite explanations of this call to love is from John, one of Jesus' closest friends. He describes how our care for others is integral to our lived-out understanding of God's love for us:

> God showed how much he loved us by sending his one and only Son into the world so that we might have eternal life through him. This is real love—not that we loved God, but that he loved us and sent his Son as a sacrifice to take away our sins. Dear friends, since God loved us that much, we surely ought to love each other. No one has ever seen God. But if we love each other, God lives in us, and his love is brought to full expression in us.
>
> 1 John 4:9–12 NLT

God's love says, *I see you. I will never leave you nor forsake you. I am an ever-present help in times of trouble. I hear your prayers. I will help carry your burdens. You are not alone.*

I can't count the number of times I have heard those words whispered in my spirit through the help of a friend. There's nothing inherently spiritual about sunflowers and ice-cream bars, but God's love was expressed to me through them.

Loving as You Go

Let's talk practical ways to serve our friends! Maybe this is new to you. Maybe no one has been this kind of friend to you or modeled well how to serve others in the middle of motherhood's craziness. Maybe you grew up with a mom who valued self-reliance over community dependence. Whether these stories of service have you nodding, *Yes! Let's do this!* or shaking your head, *No. That's not doable or even realistic,* let me put my arm around you like a sister and assure you that life-together friendships are possible, and you have what it takes to start digging in the soil of service.

Loving our friends doesn't have to be extravagant or take a lot of time or money.

One of my favorite ways to show a friend I'm thinking of her and help lighten her load is to offer to pick something up at a store I'm already going to. When you have a sick kid or a major work deadline or a hectic week of basketball games or ballet lessons, with more places to be than bodies and hours to be there, the last thing you want to do is schlepp your crew to Target for tampons and toilet paper. Whether I know someone is going through a particular trial or it's just a regular Tuesday, I ask God to put a name in my mind when I know I'm going to be out shopping. A quick text is all it takes: "Hey, you're on my heart today! I'm headed to Walmart this afternoon. Can I pick up anything for you?" Chances are your friend is going to need a loaf of bread or toothpaste or baby wipes and will be profoundly grateful you saved her a trip. Even if she says *no thanks*, the simple feeling of being thought of is a profound gift.

Another way to weave serving friends into the fabric of your life is to find manageable ways to include another kid in what you're already doing. After Jude was born, Audra asked if she could take one of the other boys with her to our moms-group playdate at the arboretum. She only had one extra spot in her car (and stroller), but she didn't let that stop her from offering help. I was more than happy to loan her Elias for a couple of hours. (If you have more than two kids, you know what a difference it makes in the family dynamic when one member is temporarily out of the picture.) Audra didn't plan a separate event; she simply made space in her day to invite one of my kids to join them.

As I nursed Jude and raced cars with Noah, I tucked Audra's gift and example in my heart. *Someday I can do this for a friend*, I thought. And I have!

During the littles years when I would take the boys to the park, I'd think of a friend I could bless with a couple of kid-free hours or at least a minus-one-kid change of pace. As my children got older, I looked for different ways to build acts of service into our life. Special trip to get frozen yogurt? Driving to baseball practice? Dropping the kids off at church for Wednesday night Awana? It doesn't take a whole lot to plan for fifteen extra minutes to swing by a friend's house and take another little (or big) person with us. But what a blessing it can be to a friend who has a napping baby or splitting headache or just wants to stay home in her pajamas.

Do you recognize the common denominator in these serving-friends scenarios? Purposely thinking of others. Gosh, that can be hard, can't it? When the baby's cutting another dagger tooth and bills are piling up and the car's transmission is on the fritz and the strong-willed child just won't quit, it's easy, and natural, to feel like you've got nothing left to give. But by sharing the weight, some of mine and some of yours and some of hers, the load is somehow more manageable. Call it a Jesus thing.

Bottom line: Don't let the thought of service freak you out. Also, don't try to be someone else.

Lean into who you are. Do what works for you! If the thought of taking another four-year-old to the park makes you twitchy, but baking bread is like therapy, don't feel obligated to offer your extra car seat; give a loaf of love instead. Maybe folding laundry is strangely soothing to you; offer to help a friend make sense of the piles of clean clothes covering her couch while the kids run wild. Are you a master at freezer meals? Love on some women by opening your home and kitchen one night to teach them how to make your favorite easy recipe.

Don't get hung up on the *what* of service—focus on the *who* and *why*. It's about blessing a friend, not being superwoman.

Using Your Unique Gifts

Last weekend I texted my friend Mindy to ask her to pray for me because I was feeling weary. School germs were in full force, Chris was out of town, there were multiple soccer games to attend and team snacks to bring, and I had an important project deadline to meet. Yeah, kind of the story of my life. But I knew even if she had heard it a hundred other times, Mindy would still care and pray. And she did. She also asked what she could do to help. Coffee? Errands? Dinner?

At 5 p.m. I found a white plastic takeout bag on my front porch with three containers of spaghetti from my favorite Italian place. *Sweet mercy!* There's hardly anything better than not having to cook dinner—at least in my book.

Food is such a practical way you can bless another mama. Don't get hung up on your culinary skills or lack thereof. If you love cooking a tasty meal from scratch, great. But there's no shame in picking up a $4.99 Costco rotisserie chicken, French baguette, and bag of salad!

Cooking is not my particular gifting. I do it because my family needs to be fed and I value healthy eating and staying on budget. I used to dread taking someone dinner. Over the years I've become less timid about it. I now have a few go-to meals to offer. If you know me in real life, you've likely eaten my turkey tacos, chili, or chicken tortilla soup. (Do you see a theme here?) Or you've received the aforementioned Costco chicken. You're welcome.

I've decided not to get down on myself for not being a foodie and instead lean into who God made me. I'm an encourager with the gift of words. That feels strange to proclaim while writing a book, but I trust you hear that I'm not tooting my own horn but calling out the way God has wired me because I want you to do the same. When a friend comes to mind, I send her a text, leave a voice message on Voxer, or grab a pen and blank card and write a quick note. I'm good at remembering what's going on in someone's life and following up to see how things turned out. I love to share a timely verse, speak a word of truth, give a compliment, say thank-you.

I laugh with Sara sometimes because I'm tempted to feel like, "Wow, so you cooked me a three-course meal and watched my son for five hours, and I gave you a note card with nice words." But she assures me, and I'm choosing to believe her, that our gifts of service don't have to be the same to be equally meaningful.

"Kind words are like honey—they cheer you up and make you feel strong" (Proverbs 16:24 CEV). What mama doesn't need some cheering and strengthening?

We grow friendships and bless others when we use the natural gifts and resources God gave us. My friends Esther and Rebecca have the ministry of back rubs. Desiree shines Jesus when she brings me iced coffee. Tracy and Elise live hundreds of miles away but serve me through their prayers over Voxer. I'm so rich in friendships I could go on and on. I could fill another chapter with examples of the diverse ways women can love one another. I once sat on a friend's bed while she showed me every item in her closet and I helped her decide what should stay and what should go (long before the days of Marie Kondo).

Several years ago I would bristle with both excitement and anxiety when I received an invitation to speak at a MOPS group. This was before Jude was in school, and he was *not* a fan of being dropped off at an unfamiliar church's child-care center. Thankfully I had a friend who wanted to help me say yes to the doors God was opening. On more than one occasion I dropped Jude off at Kyan's.

She held him when he cried as I left, took him to the library, and fed him chicken nuggets. Bless.

Do you see? Friendship isn't one size fits all, and service doesn't come with a mandatory checklist. When we intentionally view friendships as ongoing opportunities to link arms and do life together, service becomes a natural part of journeying shoulder to shoulder.

Whether you're a stellar cook or happy wordsmith, one way we can all serve our friends without cost or limit is through prayer. Don't discount the power of praying for each another. Or even better, the power of praying *with* a friend! Have you ever had a woman listen to your burden and say right there in the pew at church or the frozen food aisle or by the park swings, *Let me pray for you?* I'm not going to lie, it might feel awkward, especially if this kind of care isn't something you're used to. But let me tell you, entering into the heart space of a friend is a gift like no other.

It's great to say, "I'll pray for you" when you hear a friend's baby won't latch right or her third-grader is struggling to read or her husband got laid off. But in the whirl of motherhood, our best of prayerful intentions can fall through the cracks of busy life and forgetful minds.

Be bold, friend! You don't need fancy words. It's okay if you don't even go to church. If you believe there is a God who sees and hears and cares, then go before Him on behalf of a friend. It can be as simple as, "God, thank You for seeing my friend. Please intercede in her circumstances. Give her strength, wisdom, and peace where she needs it. Amen."

Pray with your eyes open if losing sight of your speedy toddler is a concern. The mechanics don't really matter; pausing from the rush of the day to listen, respond, and pray for one another does. The greatest gift we can give each other—better than a delectable dinner or kid-free hour—is the gift of pointing each other to Jesus.

What kind of friend do you long to have? Be her.

one simple step
Choose one to practice today.

☐ Let a friend into your mess. Be vulnerable and ask for the help you need—whether it's a meal, child care, or prayer.

☐ Call or text a friend when you're on your way to a store and ask if you can pick up something for her.

☐ When a friend shares something that is heavy on her heart, stop right then and pray with her about it.

one powerful prayer
Make this your daily prayer.

Jesus, thank You that it's not only okay to need my village, but it's how You designed us to thrive. Give me eyes to see opportunities to serve another mom in small ways this week. I trust You to grow deep friendship roots in the soil of our service. Amen.

five

Why Every Mom Deserves
a Cape

I wish I could snap my fingers and be magically transported to a coffee shop in your hometown. You would appear, and our favorite drinks would be waiting at the coziest table. Instead of the classic foam heart swirled into the frothy canvas of our lattes, there would be a different shape—a cape. You would probably do a double take and squint through your sleep-deprived eyes, not sure if you were seeing it right. Then I would lean in close and tell you what my friend and motherhood mentor Lisa-Jo Baker has been telling mamas for years: *Motherhood should come with a superhero cape.* It's true.

At this point you might shrug your shoulders or roll your eyes and then hope I didn't notice. Because very little, if anything at all, about your life feels super or heroic.

Maybe you spent your morning evaluating whether your kid's snot was still too green to qualify for child-care drop-off at the gym or church nursery. Maybe you were commiserating with friends about stretch marks and droopy boobs over waffle fries and iced coffees while your kids flapped around like screeching pterodactyls. Maybe you spent all day at the pediatrician's office trying to get the right diagnosis, or at occupational therapy praying your child would make another breakthrough, or at the Department of Child and Family Services while your foster daughter visited with her birth family. Maybe you haven't left your house in two weeks because you're trying to pump enough milk to pack your freezer before you go back to work, and your nipples are so raw you need a vat of Lanolin, stat.

I get it. And because I get it, I would lean in close, careful not to spill my coffee—I'm clumsy like that—and look you right in your beautiful, tired eyes and tell you that you're doing a remarkable job! You with the unwashed hair and five-day-old yoga pants that have never touched a yoga mat. You with the designer diaper bag and struggling spirit. You with the easy smile and hidden pain. You. Right there. You are a good mom. Not just that, you are the right mom for the job.

How do I know? Because God doesn't make mistakes. God who formed the stars and breathed life into dry bones, God who spoke the heavens into place, numbered the grains of sand, and counts the strands of wispy hair on your baby's head. The One who loved you and me and this messy world enough to save us from ourselves, our sin, by sending His precious, beloved Son to live and love and die for humankind—Him, that God, our God, doesn't make mistakes.

So if you wear the badge of mother—by planned pregnancy or unexpected blessing or the joy-pain of adoption—then you can wear it knowing your Maker made it especially for you. No mistakes. And the one who calls you Mom wasn't a mistake either. You were planned for him and he for you. You were part of her story all along. And God writes the very best stories.

Dusting Off Our Capes

As we're sipping our lattes, I'd ask you to tell me your motherhood story. I'd want to know the last thing your kid did that made your sides split with laughter. I'd want to know the thing about parenting that feels impossible. I'd tell you to pause, think, even pray, and ask yourself if there's anything in this motherhood season that makes you feel not cut out for it. Go ahead. I'll wait.

Part of the journey to fully embracing that you're the right mom for the job is being willing to call out the places in your parenting where the voice of self-doubt is louder than the song of God-confidence. What ignites insecurity for you?

Parenting in public was a constant catalyst for my confidence crashing. It's the question we can't escape when there's an audience to our mothering: *What are other people thinking?* Do they think I'm too harsh, too stern, or too strict? Am I not firm enough? Are my boundaries too rigid, too loose, or off base? Do they think I'm talking too close to my fussing child's face? I know I shouldn't get caught up in this what-are-they-thinking whirlwind, but it's easy to do in the moment. When your kid becomes *that* kid who is whining like an entitled punk because you said no to the jumbo box of Ninja Turtle fruit snacks and you're vacillating between screaming unkind things and just giving in to make the fussing stop. In *that* moment, the assumed judgment of onlooking strangers can have an unhealthy sway in what you do or say.

In public meltdown scenarios, I find that the outcome doesn't often change the way I feel about it. Whether I keep my cool or lose it, whether I come up with the right words to redirect my son and diffuse my anger or not, I still feel rotten. What sticks to my ribs and sinks in my gut in those meltdown moments is that somebody else in my mama role could do a better job. Someone else could have avoided the scene altogether. But the trouble is, there is nothing in that posture that will help me mother my kids better.

Believing that another mom would do a better job becomes like a bunch of rocks in a backpack I've doomed myself to carry. If you have any idea what I'm talking about, you know how spirit-breaking that weight can be.

My motherhood spirit was often broken because of it.

When all I could do was rest my head on the dirty shopping-cart bar and take a deep breath, begging God to make the meltdown stop, I wish I had known the words of Zephaniah 3:17: "The LORD your God is with you, the Mighty Warrior who saves. He will take great delight in you; in his love he will no longer rebuke you, but will rejoice over you with singing." The prophet who wrote this was addressing God's chosen people, assuring them that despite all the ways they made a mess of their lives and religious practices, God was still a God of hope and love and restoration; discipline was for a season, but God's delight over His people was forever.

When Jesus came to earth, lived a sinless life, died a torturous death, and was raised on the third day by God's almighty power, a new covenant was ushered in. If that sounds like religious-speak you're not fluent in, don't worry. We can say it this way: In Zephaniah's day, God's people were the Israelites—a relatively small group. Today, because of Jesus, we are all God's people! He chooses us all, which was His plan from the beginning. All we have to do is agree we've made mistakes and fallen short of God's perfect holiness; we accept that Jesus paid the price for our wrongs, ask for forgiveness, and entrust our lives to God's loving care.

This means that as God's chosen—His children—you and I get to claim all the promises of God. Read this verse again and make it personal: *The Lord my God is with me, the Mighty Warrior who saves. He will take great delight in me; in His love He will no longer rebuke me, but will rejoice over me with singing.*

That's not a picture of a God who is standing at the end of the Target aisle shaking His head and thinking I'm a failing mess. No! That's the picture of a God who is standing right there next to me. He's looking tenderly into my eyes, whispering encouragement to my heart for the one next thing I can say or do to love my kid and raise him well.

Will I recognize His voice? Will you? Chances are higher that I will when I take my gaze off the onlookers, who, let's be honest, probably don't care about my mothering tactics, and fix it squarely on the One who both promises to walk with me and has the power to equip me.

That's another assurance we can stand on: "His divine power has given us everything we need for a godly life through our knowledge of him who called us by his own glory and goodness" (2 Peter 1:3). When we feel inadequate, depleted, and ill-equipped, we can stand on the truth that God has already supplied everything we need.

Yeah, but what I actually need is more hours to close my eyes, more wisdom to make that impossible decision, more money to pay off that loan, and if the cleaning fairies could stop by my house, say, every other Wednesday, that would be great.

Is that what you're thinking? No shame in admitting it, friend. That's often the trail my thoughts travel down too. When you're in the thick of motherhood, what feels most real are the physical things around you—veggies to chop, dishes to wash, bottoms to wipe, try not to gripe. It can seem like there's a disconnect between God's promise to equip us and the concrete needs in front of us.

I need someone to burp the baby, buy the birthday present, return the library books, and figure out where that trail of ants is coming from. Can God help me with that?

"God gives us everything we need because God gives us Himself."* Parenting with confidence means letting God's song of delight become the soundtrack of our motherhood. Your circumstances may not change, but when you know—*really know*—that the God of the universe is holding your hand through every grocery store tantrum, tense parent-teacher conference, and emergency room visit, you will begin to recognize His presence. You will hear His voice more clearly, walk a little straighter, and have confidence in your true source of help.

"I lift up my eyes to the mountains—where does my help come from? My help comes from the LORD, the Maker of heaven and

---

* Ruth Chou Simons, *GraceLaced: Discovering Timeless Truths Through Seasons of the Heart* (Eugene, OR: Harvest House, 2017), 112.

earth. . . . The LORD will watch over your coming and going both now and forevermore" (Psalm 121:1–2, 8).

Yes, this is the help and hope I want to cling to in motherhood.

Therefore, I resolve not to lift my eyes to the expectations of others—perceived or real. I resolve not to rely on my own goodness or effort or ability to hold it all together. I resolve to believe that there's not a backup mom waiting in the wings ready to do my job better than me. I resolve to trust that God made me my kids' mom on purpose, for a purpose, and that He is faithful to go with us every step of this growing-up journey.

I will quit fretting and guessing and spinning my wheels wondering how another mom would handle XYZ situation. Instead, I resolve to ask: How does God want me to handle this? Where is He at work? What am I lacking that He can provide? Wisdom, patience, energy, grace? He's not in short supply! I just have to ask.

You just have to ask.

Resolutions like these have ignited a revolution in my mothering. Are you ready to resolve to make God your source of parenting confidence?

If I knew your name and address—and had copious amounts of free time—I would make it my personal mission to deliver superhero capes to every mom who reads this book. Yet I know that silky red cape wouldn't stay fastened to your neck for long. It would be quickly hijacked by your son or daughter on a mission to become their own fierce warrior. Or you'd turn it into a makeshift picnic blanket, changing pad, or swaddling cloth. Maybe it'd become a fashionable toga for your baby who had a diaper blowout in Costco, or your big kid with the sensitive gag reflex.

But wherever that red cape went, it would remind you that God's power and strength reside in you. It would remind you to be on the lookout for your unique supermom abilities.

Being on the lookout often starts by looking within.

I resolve to *trust* that God made me my kids' mom on *purpose,* for a purpose.

The Holy in the Mundane

One of the amazing things about motherhood is discovering that you have all sorts of superpowers you never knew existed. I'm not just talking about the power to soothe and nurture, provide and protect. I'm talking about the power to transform scraggly hair into a magical braided fishtail. The power to turn sheets and pillows into a dangerous dragon's lair. The power to heal grave battle wounds with nothing but two puckered lips. The power to make everyone's favorite meal with just four ingredients.

Now, you may not feel like braiding hair, building blanket forts, kissing owies, or fixing dinner are extraordinary abilities. They may not feel life altering or world changing. But what if how we *feel* about the mundane parts of motherhood isn't the best indication of the reality of our impact? Most of the things that fill up our mom days get swept into the pile of duty and responsibility. It's not like you can be an Olympic Bottom Wiper or award-winning Crushed-Cheerio Sweeper-Upper. There are no medals for getting pureed green beans out of a white onesie, no star chart for making peanut butter sandwiches every day of the week.

Though children have the same basic needs—eat, sleep, play, bathe, be hugged and loved—there is nothing basic about fulfilling them. Don't diminish the work of smashing a banana, changing pee-soaked sheets, wiggling finger puppets, or lathering up a washcloth. The way you twist pipe cleaners into a Tyrannosaurus rex for your kid's dino diorama is nothing to downplay. You made that kid's day!

Here's what I'm trying to say: One of the primary ways we believe and embrace that we're the right mom for the job is by giving proper weight to the work we do.

Look for the holy in the mundane. See the joy in the ordinary. Recognize how the little moments are not lost on your littles or on your great God whose eye never leaves you. Want to parent with confidence? Celebrate the everyday tasks. Reading books, tying shoes, changing lightbulbs, wiping the table, and washing bottles. There is beauty in making matching bows for the dance team. There is value in marveling over your athlete's lightning speed—even if his track is the backyard grass and he's only three.

Do you feel those silky strings tied around your neck? You may have spaghetti splatters on your T-shirt from last night's dinner, but there's a cape draped behind you blowing in the make-believe breeze as reminder that God made you with a host of super abilities unique to you.

The key to growing in confidence—to accepting that this proverbial cape isn't draped over your shoulders by mistake—is learning to acknowledge what you do well.

Be purposeful in thinking about your strengths as a mom.

We are all keenly aware of our weaknesses. If you came over to my house, I'd hope you wouldn't look too closely at my stove-top or breathe too deeply near the boys' toilet. I could rattle off all the things I wish I was better at as a mom: teaching my kids to read and not getting behind on laundry; how I've never been great at doing crafts or taking family portraits, and please don't tell the dentist I never floss my kids' teeth.

It's easy to let our list of weaknesses and perceived shortcomings take center stage in our minds.

Sidestepping the Comparison Peril

I found out really quickly in motherhood that if I wasn't already struggling with insecurities, dipping my toes in the pool of comparison was a surefire way to plummet further into the pit of doubt and self-pity. There are just so many ways to compare ourselves! The state of our homes and the volume of our hair. Our children's behavior, the cars we drive, how much glitter and hot glue we use. Even how many church activities we're a part of or how spiritual someone appears.

I can easily look at my friends and say: She is more patient with her kids than I am. (I struggle with anger and yelling.) She takes her kids on fun field trips. (I panic just thinking about going to a museum with my boys.) Or her kids are always color coordinated and their hair is never a wonky, bed-head mess. (Just look at us!)

I truly love social media, but if you're on Facebook or Instagram, you know that, for the most part, we're all putting up a highlight reel instead of a complete picture of life's blessings *and* struggles. The result of this is that we end up pitting our known weaknesses against someone else's perceived strengths. What good is that? If you find yourself saying, "I should be more like so-and-so," it's like telling God He messed up making you.

Many people will call this type of thinking the comparison trap. Can we pause for one quick second and address that? I think we should decide not to use that term anymore. Comparison trap. It sounds like some sneaky, sinister scheme just waiting to devour us. Like there's no way we can avoid it. *It's not my fault I think or feel this way; it's the comparison trap! It got me—again.* Do you see what I mean? Instead, try out the phrase *comparison peril*. It still reminds us that comparison is dangerous. But who is in control of putting ourselves in perilous situations? We are.

Let's take responsibility for our thought life and how it impacts our confidence as parents.

With that said, we can acknowledge that there are many "types" of moms. You may not be the doing-crafts-with-your-kids mom, or the cooking-organic-gluten-free-meals mom, or the don't-let-your-kids-watch-TV-because-you're-teaching-them-to-knit mom. (I'm definitely not that last mom.) But that doesn't mean that you aren't exactly the mom *your* kid needs!

Still having a hard time believing it? Oh, friend, I get it. When your child is going through a season of defiance or constant disobedience, when she's having trouble making friends at school or there is drama on the baseball field, when you simply feel stretched in too many directions, it's hard to believe that you really are cut out for being their mom. I've been there. Many days I *am* there!

So in the thick of motherhood's toughest seasons, how do we practically embrace that we're the exact mom God designed for our kids? Identify what you are really good at.

Celebrate Your Strengths

This idea first crossed my mind when I was preparing a new talk for a MOPS group. I thought, *Yeah, identifying what you're good at is a great way to deal with feelings of inadequacy and awaken to the beautiful ways God has wired you.* Then it occurred to me that if I was going to preach this to other mamas, I should probably live it first. Shoot. The exercise was harder than I'd like to admit.

This was several years ago when my kids were probably five, four, and two. Here's what my list at the time looked like:

Things I'm good at as a mom:
- Encouraging creativity—helping my kids turn everyday items into imaginative play: cardboard boxes into spaceships, bushes into soldier forts, empty paper towel rolls into light sabers.
- Cultivating thankfulness—asking every day what we're grateful for, making bedtime prayers a list of thanks, showing the boys my gratitude journal.
- Providing healthy food—hiding veggies in pasta sauce, fried rice, and chili.
- Making up crazy songs—all. day. long.
- Showing physical affection—hugs, kisses, cuddles, back scratches, tickles.

I made this list without letting myself think, *Well, everybody does that.* My mom strengths have nothing to do with other people—neither do yours! Don't discount what you do well. Don't believe that every mom does what you do.

103

I'll never forget that first moms group I shared this talk with. I asked for someone from the audience to share one thing she was good at as a mom. The room had never been so quiet. Finally, one mom reluctantly raised her hand. Her name was Emilee.

"I guess I'm good at sticking to my guns and following through on consequences," she said.

Emilee went on to describe a recent trip to Disneyland when her daughter's behavior was less than stellar on the drive down. I don't recall what the exact issue was, but this mom made it clear to her little girl that if she continued doing what she was told not to, they would immediately leave the Magic Kingdom—no more warnings or eighteenth chances.

That mom and her two kids finished the drive. They parked in the crowded lot near Pluto or Buzz Lightyear. They took the shuttle and walked the long walk and waited in the long admission line until they finally went through the metal turnstile, flashed their annual passes, and entered the gates. Once inside the theme park, they met up with friends at their planned spot. What fun to spend the day with another mom and her kids in the Happiest Place on Earth!

Then, as they were making their way to the very first ride of the day, Emilee's daughter did that thing her mother had told her not to.

"So we left," the mom in front of me said.

I'm pretty sure my mouth wasn't the only one agape. I'm pretty sure I started applauding right there for the grit and resolve that mama showed. If sticking to your guns isn't a superpower, I don't know what is!

To Emilee, this story was ordinary. It represented a frustrating parenting moment marked by all the inconvenience and hassle of wishing your kid would just *learn the lesson,* but following through on the consequence anyway. But to me and all the women gathered in that church meeting room, there was nothing ordinary about it.

I assured her that not every mom is good at sticking to her guns. (Hand raised sheepishly high.) Sure, I could have had the same conversation in the car. I would have clearly explained to my kid the behavior expectations and the resulting consequence should another deliberate infraction be made. But make no mistake, the outcome would have been different. With all the effort I put in to getting to Disneyland and the weight of a friend's expectation riding on my back, I have no doubt that I would have either (a) pretended to ignore my child's disobedience or (b) made ugly threats under my breath about the punishment waiting at home should he do it again. *Now, who wants to go on Thunder Mountain?*

I realize this isn't putting myself in a very good light. But the point isn't predicting how I would *not* have stuck to my guns, but celebrating how this beautiful mama did! Had Emilee not been brave enough to name her strength, she probably wouldn't have realized how extraordinary it is.

What you do every hour of every day as a mother is amazing. Yet it's so commonplace, it's hard to recognize the wonder.

Magnify the Wonder

It reminds me of people who live in snowy climates. As a California girl, I think snow is magical. Once, maybe twice a year, we'll drive up to our local mountains, build a lopsided snowman, and cackle as the boys slide down snowdrifts on their neon-green saucers. I'll listen closely to the crunching sound beneath my boots. Then look up and behold a pine tree thick with snow. I marvel at the way ice crystals have encapsulated evergreen needles. I slowly orbit around the living skyscraper, taking in the way the glisten changes with every angle, like nature's disco ball. But my mama friend in Minnesota who lives for months in the snow probably doesn't find the frozen landscape nearly as magical. She has to deal with snow-day school cancellations, frozen pipes, and never-ending piles of winter gear.

Whether winter weather is a novelty or an everyday inconvenience, put a single snowflake under a microscope and no one can deny the glory. If you've never seen the miracle, hop on your computer or smartphone, and google *snowflake photography*. Scroll in awestruck wonder over the intricate, one-of-a-kind beauty of each of these crystalline creations. Talk about undeniably amazing!

Likewise, it takes intentionally zooming in on our ordinary responsibilities to see with fresh eyes the unique beauty we bring to motherhood. All the snowflakes together just look like a pile of frozen white fluff. It's the same way with motherhood. When all our daily mothering tasks and routines are lumped together, the picture can look like just a Lego-strewn living room and dish-piled kitchen.

It's our job to put motherhood under the microscope of close attention.

Don't look at that whole toy-bombed playroom. Pick up just one piece. Like a doll. Remember how you French-braided her red yarn hair. Remember the delight in your daughter's eyes when she saw her beautiful princess. Recall the story you dreamed up together and the way you stacked couch cushions to make a castle tower. Or turn your gaze to the kitchen and put a macro lens on that muffin tin. Remember how your son helped heap in a spoonful of cinnamon and the joy he had mixing all the ingredients with the big wooden spoon. See the flour dusting his nose. Take in the wonder of you, the one who said yes to teaching your kid to measure sugar and crack an egg.

Since the day I heard Emilee's mom-strength story, I've spoken to thousands of mothers. I continue to implore them with the same encouragement: Identify what you do well and celebrate it!

As moms, we are acutely aware of all the ways we fall short, miss the mark, and don't measure up. We can rattle off a list longer than our Amazon wish list of all the areas we could do more, try harder, be better as a mother. Admitting our weaknesses comes easy. It's much harder to name our strengths.

In recent months, as I've given more of myself to work and writing, the voice of "you're not enough as a mom" has been slowly getting louder. Maybe that's a lie that's taken root in your heart too. As a way of reclaiming the truth—that God did not make a mistake in making me my kids' mom—I'm going to again call out the simple, beautiful, regular, extraordinary things that are my unique mom superpowers:

- I make living-room-movie picnics like a boss—individual blankets, plastic trays, frozen pizzas, cut fruit. Bam.
- I have a terrible singing voice, but my boys all still ask for their bedtime song and only like the way I sing it.
- I know exactly how each kid likes their preferred version of a breakfast burrito, a peanut butter sandwich, and chicken tacos.
- I give the tightest hugs and best squirrel kisses.
- I have a robust stamina for card games.
- I bring snacks at school pickup, and I fill up sports bottles with just the right amount of ice and water.
- I apply essential oils to upset tummies and magically produce socks when all are seemingly dirty or lost.

That's me—Noah, Elias, and Jude's mom. I love my boys more than lava is hot, a cave is dark, and a tree is tall. At the end of each imperfect day, I think that's all that really matters.

If you're constantly comparing yourself to others, slogging through the bog of insecurity, or feeling like a flat-out mom failure, focus on the things that make you distinctly *you* as a mother. I dare you!

It could be as small as brushing tiny teeth or trimming bangs. What about the way you teach the ABCs or whisper that bedtime prayer? Do you know the perfect way to put on socks without forming any bumps? Do you take your family on nature walks to find red leaves? Are you a whiz in science or robotics and show your kids how to do cool things with radios and batteries? Do you grow a garden and let your kids plant seeds? Do you keep family activities organized in color-coded wonder and make sure everyone is at the right place at the right time while driving carpool with a smile?

Our imaginary lattes are almost empty. I'm sipping slowly because I don't want our coffee date to end. I want to hear all about the way you grease a squeaky scooter and masterfully fold the impossible fitted sheet. I want you to tell me about how you advocate for your son with special needs and are relentlessly committed to getting your daughter with the daunting diagnosis the very best treatment. I'd love to know how you stretch every dollar to feed your army of children and all their hungry neighborhood friends. I want to know what it's like to have an only child and how you shuffle between the hats of mama and best friend.

But more than anything I want you to tell it all to *yourself*. I want you to listen to the story of your life. Marvel over every detail of your mothering like you would for a dear friend. Then say, "That's me! Those are my gifts. This is how I love my child well."

Yes it is. Yes it is. Yes it is.

Breathe deep, dear sister. God delights over you.

- -

one simple step
Choose one to practice today.

☐ When you have a public parenting blunder, picture God right next to you. Ask Him for wisdom. Remember that He picked you to parent your kid.

☐ Write a list of your unique mom strengths. When insecurity creeps in, read that list out loud—as many times as you need to believe it. (If you're really brave, share that list with a friend!)

☐ Look for the wonder in an ordinary moment. Slow down and feel the pleasure of mothering your child well.

. . . .

one powerful prayer
Make this your daily prayer.

Jesus, help me to know more deeply the delight You feel for me. Help me understand the great weight of Your love by seeing the great ways You've equipped me to be my kid's mom. Thank You for my one-of-a-kind superpowers. I can mother with confidence because You are with me. Amen.

six

When the People You Love the Most Bring Out Your Worst

I pulled treasures out of a high cupboard and set Noah and Elias up for a few minutes of independent play. Strategic stashing of forgotten toys was one of my favorite mommy tricks to occupy toddlers with the novelty of "new" and buy myself a little time. Content with their red monster trucks and ABC blocks, I left my two-year-old and three-year-old on the living room rug, picked up the baby, and hurried to my bedroom.

Today, I was going to get dressed. Pants without an elastic waistband, a shirt without spit-up. This was big stuff.

I looked through every pair of jeans in my drawer and every shirt in my closet and they all screamed *awkward*! I was still in that uncomfortable postpartum stage where neither maternity clothes nor my old skinny jeans were an appropriate fit. I glanced at Jude drooling happily in his bouncy seat, swatting at the fuzzy monkeys hanging from the mobile. Cheerful noises drifted from the living room.

"Brudder, do you wanna race me?" The zoom of toy wheels racing over hardwood floors and the familiar crash of plastic against baseboards echoed through the house.

"Boys," I called, "I'm so glad you're playing nicely! Keep up the good work."

After examining every piece of clothing a second time (and perhaps trying on half a dozen disheartening combinations), I decided a fresh pair of yoga pants was probably the best choice. I pulled on the comforting, stretchy fabric and reached for a flowy top. It wasn't as cute an outfit as I had hoped, but I wasn't going anywhere special. I just wanted to feel more normal. Less frumpy. More woman and less milk machine.

Then I noticed it was very quiet. I *love* quiet. Pray for it, give thanks for it, deeply cherish any moment of silence I can get. But quiet is rarely a good sign with young boys. I peeked my head out the door and peered into the living room. No little bodies to be found. I heard a giggle. After a few steps, I spied skinny legs crouching under the dining room table.

"Whatchya doing under there?" I asked.

"Umm . . . nothing?" my oldest replied.

I crouched down to look in the faces of my mischievous children. I was not prepared for what I saw.

Wedged between their feet lay an open egg carton. Correction: an *empty* egg carton. Cracked shells. Yolks everywhere. STICKY SALMONELLA SLIME SLIDING DOWN THEIR ARMS! It had been a full dozen, and they broke every single one.

I instantly transformed into Monster Mommy. Crimson face, raging pulse pounding in my ears, I roared angry disapproval at my boys at a decibel my hard-of-hearing neighbor could probably hear. With white knuckles, I clenched the arm of each eggy offender and escorted them to the bathtub.

"Sit down and don't you dare move!"

I seethed, picking fragments of jagged shell out of the looped carpet. I could hear the boys sobbing as I sopped up the yellow pond of wastefulness.

When I returned to the bathroom, they didn't dare to ask for a rubber ducky or superhero figure. I didn't care enough to wait for the water to warm to their preferred temperature before scrubbing my boys vigorously. It wasn't even 8 a.m.

Just as I was beginning to regain my composure, I found egg smeared on my clean outfit. I imploded.

Seven years later, I can laugh over the ridiculousness of this event. Shaking my head, I smile with affection over how my boys were just being curious kids and I was just an exhausted mom reacting to an unfortunate episode of childhood mayhem. But for days, maybe even weeks after the incident, I beat myself up over how I had completely lost it. I carried a thick blanket of guilt over the way I had scary-screamed at my small children. I felt shame over the hot tears we all cried—tears springing more from my volatile response than their poor choice.

An Honest Confession

I know most people would offer the comfort and consolation that I was *normal*. That anyone would react that way to food being wasted and a good rug being ruined. Not to mention the sheer aggravation of cleaning up raw egg goop. And it was normal for kids to occasionally do absurdly maddening things. Impulses are hard to control and curiosity is a powerful thing. Yet, calling it "normal" didn't bring relief to my shame-wounded heart. Because this wasn't an isolated incident.

I was angry a lot. And not just about big stuff like children crushing eggs into my dining room carpet.

If a boy fussed about buckling his car seat or asked for a second bedtime drink. If brothers bickered over whose turn it was to use the blue crayon or someone dropped a bowl of Cheerios on a freshly swept floor. If a little one wanting attention tapped my shoulder or tugged my shirt *just one more time*—I was like a time bomb waiting to go off. From calm and clear-minded to triggered. Boom! Explosive.

I was a young mom with three kids under four who was rocked raw that the very people I loved the most could bring out my very worst. Have you stomached this heartbreaking experience? Admitting that the precious ones you treasure, the children you delight in, the kid you would literally lay down your life for has become the unexpected key to unlocking the Pandora's box of all your secret ugliness?

Before becoming a mom, I liked to consider myself a pretty stable person. I was reasonable. In control. Never volatile, except for one memorable nasty fight with my sister when we were kids, a few less-than-stellar PMS moments, and that time I yelled at my college roommate for smacking her mac and cheese too loudly while I was trying to study. (I'm sorry, Sarah. I still feel bad about that. Apparently, misophonia is a real thing.) But in the scope of three decades, I'd call that a pretty fair track record.

I never considered I had a problem with anger—until I had kids.

I'm sure all the gunk in my heart was building up before I ever gave birth. But I never knew how utterly selfish, irritated, irate, bitter, fed up, anxious, depressed, disillusioned, and entitled I could be until my precious cherubs came along and innately knew how to pull the lever that unleashed it all. Whoosh. Floodgates of ugly released. *How do they do that?*

Maybe this isn't your story. Perhaps you take the exhaustion and chaos and strain of motherhood in stride. Maybe it comes naturally to you to respond calmly instead of react harshly. Not that you don't get mad. But being frustrated and being out of control are two very different things. If you don't relate to flat-out losing it with your kids, I'm genuinely grateful for you and with you—that is a gift, and you are gold! But please don't tune out this chapter. Even if you don't struggle with anger, chances are you have a friend who does.

Listen closely because you just might learn something that could be a lifeline of hope to someone else. You might not guess your friend has rage boiling beneath the surface by the sweet spirit and soothing voice you observe—in public. Behind closed doors can be a very different story. I've talked to too many moms to believe that I'm the only one who feels fried and frayed and undone by being a sometimes-angry mom.

I'll beat this drum as long and loud as it takes for every mom to hear it: We must be willing to take our struggles out of the darkness of isolation and into the light of shared experience. Our confidence shrinks in the shadows of guilt and shame. Insecurity grows in the dark corners of feeling like you're the only one who deals with fill-in-the-blank.

At the height of my battle with anger (and *battle* isn't too strong a word), I felt totally unfit to mother my children. Even though I *knew* I was a good mom, my anger made me feel disqualified. I knew I cut sandwiches into triangles and applied Elmo Band-Aids to scraped knees. I dipped jagged fingernails and applied the right diaper cream and read the same board book twenty more times. I was tender and attentive and present. Yet. Yet when a kid hit his brother or woke up too early or smooshed Play-Dough on the couch pillows or asked for a snack twelve times after I already said *no*, I might just lose it. Snap. Yell. Bark. Lecture-wail.

Every angry outburst became like a chalkboard eraser, blurring the lines of all the good and right I had done until it was just a mess of white powder. Poof. Confidence gone.

No matter how many good-mom things I did, the sheer shame over my angry outbursts became like a thick blanket of failure that I couldn't get out from under. You know what helped pull back a corner? A friend who was willing to tell me I wasn't alone. A friend who was willing to take a flashlight of truth to my dark shadows and remind me of the whole picture of who I am as a mom and whose I am as God's daughter.

I am loving and loved. Even in my anger. And so are you.

So lean in here, mama. Be a safe place for a friend to admit the daily battle she's fighting and the oppressive guilt she's carrying. Whether you relate to mommy anger or not, you can be a greater gift to a struggling friend than you might imagine.

That One Time We All Cried

I remember the first time I *really* lost it. This was before the egg-crushing incident. Jude must have been about six weeks old, because it was during the eight dark weeks that descended upon us like an unrelenting storm when he had colic. As a newborn, Jude was great. His first month of life was beautiful. Then, bam—inconsolable crying overcame him like a plague. It didn't lift for two solid months.

If Jude was awake, he was screaming. Nonstop. Noah and Elias started covering their ears with whatever plush toy or spare hand they had.

It had been a particularly rough day. I can't even tell you the specifics. The peripheral details have faded with the fog of time, but I can see with laser-like clarity the replay of the epic scene that unfolded. Watch it with me:

After thirty-seven attempts (and failures) to get the baby to stop crying—swing, stroller, car ride, bouncy seat, gas drops, infant massage, and on and on—an exhausted mother finally gets her infant wrapped snugly in the black Moby contraption. After pleading prayers and endless tries, she discovers the right combination of bounce-shimmy-sway and rhythmically dances the screaming child into silence. She's sweaty with effort, but the baby finally drifts off to sweet slumber. *Thank You, Jesus!*

It is the middle of July and one hundred degrees outside. The AC in the little blue rental house is less than stellar. Wrapping oneself in multiple layers of tightly wound black fabric to insulate a cozy baby who is already like a portable human heater is not a delightful experience. But the baby is sleeping. And the mama sings silent hallelujahs.

She can finally breathe.

The mom tiptoes through the house, careful to avoid the creaky hall floorboards. She motions to her two toddler sons to sit on the couch.

"You can watch *Dinosaur Train* while the baby sleeps," she whispers.

She turns the TV on low and finds the colorful cartoon on Netflix as the little boys scamper up on the couch. The baby is now breathing steadily, and the mama sighs with relief. Even with the catchy songs and entertaining storyline, the wise mama knows that her boys will not be content for long. She creeps to the kitchen to retrieve a midmorning snack. She scours the fridge and pantry for something that is quiet to gather and relatively clean to eat.

Ahh, mini raisin boxes and special-occasion applesauce squeeze packs for the win!

She comes around the corner to deliver the surprise snacks and discovers an empty couch. Both boys stand directly in front of the TV.

"Sit back down, please," she whispers.

"Can't find the remote. I need it louder!" Noah declares, finger probing the black rim of the TV, searching for the manual volume control.

"It's loud enough. Jude is sleeping," the mom's whisper elevates.

"Louder, Mommy, louder."

"No. Shhh. . . . Boys, sit down."

"But Mommy . . ."

All the while the mother bounces and sways, lest the baby wake and return to screaming. She adjusts the fabric to make sure it's in proper support position.

She finally notices Elias's incessant pointing. Grinning and pointing. But not at the TV.

"What *is* it, Elias?"

"Pee pee! Pee pee!"

The mother's gaze falls to the floor and sees the puddle in which her children are standing. The puddle on the wood floor that is almost touching the living room rug while spreading dangerously close to the electrical power strip underneath the entertainment stand.

Yet in her split-second assessment she is confused. *Did Noah drop a cup of water?* Her three-year-old was fully potty trained and her just-turned-two-year-old was still diapered. *Did Elias take off his diaper?* No, she spies the telltale bulges under his cotton shorts. *Did it leak?* But this isn't a dribble. This is a lake.

"Noah, pee pee! Noah, pee pee!" the middle brother cheers before his mama can ask the question.

"Noah! What happened?" she gasps. "How did you have an accident?"

"I didn't want to miss the show," he admits, eyes still glued to the talking dinosaurs.

Had she been wearing a heart rate monitor, chances are it would have been beeping with extreme cardio activity.

"Stay *right* there. Do not move. Either of you."

The mom tosses the raisin boxes and applesauce pouches on the couch and goes to the bathroom to grab a towel. Seven seconds later she returns to the living room . . . and she sees it. Her children are jumping. Jumping and splashing in the puddle of pee! Urine droplets launch in every direction, making contact with the rug, the DVD player, the TV screen.

The mother forgets everything that has happened before this moment. She forgets that her third child is secured to her body. All she can do is scream. Oh, and she screams.

"STOP RIGHT NOW!!" erupts from deep in her gut.

The pee-er cries. The companion splasher cries. The baby goes from sleeping to wailing in two seconds flat. And the exhausted mommy falls in a heap on the floor and sobs.

This picture remains like a screaming still-frame for a long time. Boys standing in pee crying. Baby wrapped in black, his tiny red face howling. Mom paralyzed by anger and shame and sweat dripping between her boobs and down her back.

Is it bedtime yet?

Seven years have passed, and I can chuckle at the tragic comedy that was/is my life. I want to reach back in time and hand that mama an extra towel. I want to hug that younger me and tell her it's okay to cry. It's okay that motherhood is hard. It's okay to fail. It's okay to throw the pee towels in the washer, put the crying baby in the crib, and wash your hands and face. Then go back out, sit those boys down on the couch, and tell them that jumping in pee is a poor choice and so is Mommy yelling.

I want to assure her that she's doing her imperfect best and that's all the Lord expects.

I want to remind her that God sees the way she crouches down and looks straight in the faces of the little ones who call her mama.

He sees the way she says, "I'm so sorry for screaming at you. I was really upset, but I should have taken a deep breath and used my words instead. I see that I hurt your feelings and I scared you. That was wrong of me. Will you please forgive me?"

She feels like it's not enough—the damage outweighs the apology. She doesn't realize that God has control of the scales and He tips things in favor of our refining and redemption. She doesn't believe that the good her sons are learning about brokenness and forgiveness, about what it looks like to miss the mark and need God's grace, is perhaps a greater lesson than could be gleaned from a mother who never faltered—or hid it when she did.

Friend, God was not angry at me then, or me today, or you yesterday, or right this moment, or when you mess up tomorrow. He doesn't lose His cool the way we lose ours. Yes, there is a righteous anger to God's character. He wants us to love well and steward the gifts and responsibilities He's given us with wisdom and grace. But I don't think He's shooting down lightning bolts of shame at mothers all over the world when they snap at their kids or even monster-mommy yell in messy, incredulous moments involving bodily fluids. God is our Father. He understands how children can be—immature, in process, growing up as they go.

God has control
of the *scales*
and He tips things
in favor of our
refining and
redemption.

I think if God had flesh on today, He would pull a warm quilt out of the dryer and wrap me and my boys up in a big group hug. He'd pat our backs and pet our hair and let us lay our heads on His sturdy chest. He'd welcome us to cry or sleep for a good long while.

He offers the same comfort and assurance to you and your kids too.

> Through the heartfelt mercies of our God,
> God's Sunrise will break in upon us,
> Shining on those in the darkness,   •
> those sitting in the shadow of death,
> Then showing us the way, one foot at a time,
> down the path of peace.
>
> Luke 1:78–79 MSG

I write this today as a testament to God's redeeming grace. I am not the same mom I was those days my kids crushed that carton of eggs and splashed urine all over the TV. Do I never get triggered? Is my anger completely gone? Not by a long shot. I am still very much in process. But I have made meaningful progress.

Looking back, I recognize three main things the Lord used to help me break through my sin of anger:

1. Being rooted in the Word and prayer.
2. Getting honest with and accountable to friends.
3. Inviting my kids into the process of forgiveness and fresh starts.

At the root of my anger was my desire to be in control. This is ironic, of course, because as soon as I allowed anger to overtake my thoughts, emotions, and behavior, I became decidedly out of control. The seething, screaming, teeth-gritting Monster Mommy was driving the show. The ensuing scene was never pretty or predictable.

At times I felt entitled to my anger—as awful as that is to admit. Like, wouldn't anyone in my shoes be destined to lose it? Wouldn't anyone come undone after being repeatedly ignored, blatantly disobeyed, and having your favorite coffee creamer spilled all over the floor by a freakishly strong toddler who broke the fridge lock? And when you're going on only a few hours of highly interrupted sleep, forget about it. You've heard of being hangry (hungry and angry). Aren't all moms doomed to be sleepy angry—*slangry*?

When an angry outburst was continually boiling just below the surface, I didn't want to take responsibility for my reactions. It's so much easier to maintain a victim mentality. Like, this is happening to me. It's unfortunate that it spills over to my kids, but there's not a whole lot I can do about it. I guess I'll just wait till we all grow up.

Clearly, this plan wasn't going to work. I had to own that what I was doing wasn't working. My anger was not in line with God's plan for my parenting. I was the adult who needed to change.

In the thick of my battle with anger, one of the first verses I ever memorized came back to mind: "Don't copy the behavior and customs of this world, but let God transform you into a new person by changing the way you think. Then you will learn to know God's will for you, which is good and pleasing and perfect" (Romans 12:2 NLT). *A new person.* Yes. That's what I wanted, what I desperately needed.

A New Way of Thinking

I knew I couldn't control my anger by my own sheer grit—tried that and failed. Sure, getting more sleep would improve the situation, but I couldn't bank on that happening as a mom of young children. I needed something outside myself, something steady and faithful in the midst of my turbulent and unpredictable.

I needed to be transformed by Jesus.

But how would He, could He, do it? "Let God transform you into a new person *by changing the way you think.*" God wanted my thoughts.

My thoughts were consumed with a whole lot of me. I constantly thought about how tired and fatigued I was. I thought about my daily frustrations and how I wished my kids were calmer and more compliant. This thinking quickly spiraled out of control like a toddler coming down from a red-dye sugar high: *This life is so hard. Why won't they listen? I feel so underappreciated and disrespected!*

These thoughts weren't helping me or my kids. I needed a new way of thinking.

All Scripture is God-breathed and is useful for teaching, rebuking, correcting and training in righteousness, so that the servant of God may be *thoroughly equipped for every good work.*

2 Timothy 3:16–17, emphasis mine

Right there God promises to equip us for every good work. Surely the work of motherhood qualifies. But oh, how ill-equipped I can feel, especially in the throes of an angry meltdown. Have you been there?

There is no greater lifeline, no better source for renewing our minds than the Word of God. If we want to parent with confidence, we have to make Scripture the most important thing we carry. More than diapers, Band-Aids, granola bars, Hot Wheels, hand sanitizer, random crayons, gum, a sunscreen stick, and emergency Starbucks gift card, we need God's truth within reach.

The Bible says that *all* Scripture is useful for equipping us, but my maxed-out mama brain couldn't retain all of it.

Here are just three Scriptures I used like anchors.

- "A gentle answer turns away wrath, but a harsh word stirs up anger" (Proverbs 15:1).

- "My dear brothers and sisters, take note of this: Everyone should be quick to listen, slow to speak and slow to become angry, because human anger does not produce the righteousness that God desires" (James 1:19–20).

- "But the fruit of the Spirit is love, joy, peace, forbearance, kindness, goodness, faithfulness, gentleness and self-control" (Galatians 5:22–23).

I wrote these verses on index cards and taped them to the cabinet next to the kitchen sink. I read them every time I prepped a meal or washed a dish. I wrote them on sticky notes and put them on my laptop. I read them before I checked email or sat down to work. I wrote them in my journal and left the page turned open. Slowly God's Word moved from ink on pale-yellow Post-it squares to convictions etched deep in my heart.

The next time Elias dumped an entire box of cereal on the hardwood floor and Noah took it as an opportunity to stomp like he was popping bubble wrap, the words *joy*, *gentleness*, and *self-control* became like a fire extinguisher to my anger.

Be slow to become angry, I whispered to myself as I handed Elias a trash bag and Noah a dustpan.

This is the gift of God's Word. It is alive and active (Hebrews 4:12). It's not just ancient advice on modern pages; Scripture is timeless truth with the power to transform our hearts and minds. It has the power to transform our motherhood.

Whether yelling is your primary mode of communication or you succumb to the occasional angry outburst, make a choice today to renew your mind with God's Word and let Him change the way you think.

Choose one of the verses above, or find one that resonates with you. Write it on a sticky note. Put it where you'll see it. Read it. Every day. Read it as often as you warm up a bottle or Velcro little shoes or check Instagram.

The way we think is the guiding force to the way we behave.

Being vulnerable with a friend can also help loosen the grip of your anger and shame. There is power in admitting out loud that you don't want to keep living angry.

Find a friend who will love you in your ugly and point you to the One who accepts you, forgives you, and can transform you. Be that kind of friend for someone else.

Snap a photo of that Scripture card by your kitchen sink or on your bathroom mirror and send it to another mama. Chances are, if you need that mind-renewing truth, your friend does too. When you're on the verge of slamming a door or screaming at your kid, take a mini timeout. Walk into another room or sit on the back porch for thirty seconds. Take a deep breath. Cry out to God for the right words, the right perspective, and the wisdom He promises (James 1:5). Then text a friend. Name your struggle. Write out what brought you to the boiling-over point. Decide the right response you want to have. Ask her to pray as you do it.

Don't underestimate the gift of walking this out in community.

Why Our Mess-Ups Matter

It's also good to invite our kids into our transformation journey. We have the opportunity to not only train our kids with love and gentleness, but also to model what it looks like to mess up well—to apologize sincerely and ask for forgiveness. This is not easy in the heat of the moment. When you're staring at a child's face red with defiance, when you're fighting back your own hot tears, saying "I'm sorry. Please forgive me" can feel as natural as choking on sand.

Our kids don't need our wrath. They also don't need our false perfection. Tuck these phrases into your heart for the next time you miss the mark:

Mommy messed up.
I was wrong for yelling.

125

I'm sorry for being harsh.

I should have used calm words.

Will you forgive me?

Let's start over.

These simple words have nothing to do with correcting our kid's behavior. That can come later. This is about modeling our own need to take responsibility and seek forgiveness. I can't tell you how many times my kids have been quick with a genuine "I'm sorry" because I was willing to go first. Saying sorry to our kids when we blow it and blow up doesn't excuse their poor behavior. If they did wrong, that needs to be addressed. But our wrong does too.

There's also something surprising that happens when we show our kids that we're on the same team. Teammates have to help each other do their part better.

I remember one day feeling flat-out fed up and spent. All my angry words, all my calm corrections, none of it seemed to make a difference to kids who just wouldn't listen. No matter what I said or how I said it, their behavior was staying the same and my frustration was growing bigger than the overflowing laundry baskets (and that's big).

My kids were about eight, seven, and five at the time, and I sat them all down on the bed and was brutally honest. I recounted all the ways they hadn't listened. I told them how sad and frustrated it makes me when I give clear instructions: stop the wrestling and tickle wars, stop using stuffed animals as weapons, and start calming down for bedtime. I told them again how sorry I was for yelling. Then I said something new.

"How can I help you listen?" I asked. "How can I help you obey?"

They wiggled and fidgeted and flopped on the bed. I reminded them again to sit up and look me in the eyes.

I'm not sure what I was expecting, but I wasn't expecting what they said next.

"Play another card game with us," my oldest offered.

"Sit on the couch with me and read me a story and then I'll say all the words back to you," my youngest said.

And the middle guy with the hottest temper and biggest heart threw himself in my lap and just cried, "I'm sorry for not listening to you, Mommy."

I often think my kids just need more time to play outside, more freedom to explore. I imagine that if we lived on open land, they'd get all their crazy energy out by turning fallen trees into forts and then come inside and be well behaved. Sure, there's something to that. Yes, we love any chance we get to enjoy nature. But that night I was reminded that the nature of my boys isn't just to run wild; they were also made to be nurtured. While they're still responsible for their behavior (as I am for mine), maybe they just need more of me.

When I started writing this book, I told God I didn't want new material. Which was my super secret code for *God, please don't make me learn any new lessons or endure any new trials that will be pertinent to this message.*

Turns out God isn't big into bargaining.

Today I got new material.

We were driving home from summer sports camp when Jude asked me to turn on some music. With the push of a button, the most recent VBS soundtrack filled the minivan with Jesus-praising peppy beats. Elias started to sing. Noah started to complain. I turned up the music a few more notches, hoping the volume would drown out both of their voices enough to usher in thumping harmony for the short ride home.

Mere inches separated their faces as all three boys smooshed together in the back, making me loathe the fact that we had never gotten around to reinstalling the second-row seats we removed for a recent camping trip. Personal space is always our friend. A lack thereof is not.

Elias sang louder, off-key. Noah covered his ears in exaggerated annoyance.

Then came the kind of whining that achieves a tone and decibel uniquely capable of piercing a mother's soul.

"Eliiiii! Stooopppp iiiiitt!"

"I'm just singing. Stop plugging your ears. That's ruuuuude, Noaaah!"

"You're too loud. You're hurting my ears! It's so annoying."

"I'm worshiping God. You think worshiping God is annoying?"

"No, I think YOU'RE annoying."

"Well, I think you're the rudest brother ever, and I'm never going to stop singing ever."

"I just want some peace and quiet. Sing it in your head!" Noah said louder.

"I like singing out loud and you're ruining my worship!"

"Mooooommmm, make Elias stop!"

"Mooooommmy, tell Noah to stop being mean!"

And on . . . and on . . . and on . . . until I wouldn't have been surprised to catch a glimpse of my reflection in the rearview mirror and see blood dripping from my ears. (I have no idea where my children get their dramatic flair.)

As I type out this little scene in the serenity of my local Coffee Bean & Tea Leaf, the whole thing now seems slightly comical. Brothers bickering over their preferred method of enjoying Christian children's music. *Come on. Get a grip, little people.*

In the moment I could have laughed at the scene. I could have turned down the music, validated their feelings, and called out their unkindness. Maybe I should have pulled over and crawled into the back seat so I could look them in the eyes and say something really spiritual and wise about how worshiping God can look different for different people and what makes God's heart happiest is when we treat one another with love and respect. I could have, should have done a lot of things.

Instead, I grabbed that black volume knob and whipped it to the left, lest no Christian lyrics compete with the impending announcement of my displeasure.

"Knock it off! Both of you!" I boomed. "You are *both* being rude and annoying. I can't stand the way you guys fight! It's distracting when I'm driving and totally selfish. Why don't you think about someone other than yourself for once?!"

I seethed in my seat as they sulked in theirs.

When those last words came out, I meant them about each child, that my children should be more loving and think about their brother instead of their own desires. But really? Really, I wanted them to think more about me.

As they were jockeying for their preferred music experience, feeling entitled to having it *their way,* I was battling my own entitlement. I preferred peace. Easy peace. I didn't want to spend the sweaty July car ride training my children to communicate their feelings, compromise, and choose a kind response even when irritated. My head was full of details for a work project and travel logistics for an upcoming trip—and I felt entitled to the kind of interruption-free drive conducive to deep thinking.

Lashing out at my kids was my version of competing for what was best for me. Ugh. The mirror of selfishness glared back at me.

Friend, I want to be over all of this. I want to respond rightly to my kids the first time, every time. I want a relentlessly calm and even-tempered demeanor and an endless reservoir of patience. I want to always parent with the big picture in mind instead of reacting out of in-the-moment frustration. So, umm . . . I kind of want to be perfect.

Yet I know that perfection isn't the point to parenting. I know being free from flaws and never messing up isn't a reasonable expectation—for anyone. I'll happily tell a friend till my voice is hoarse what a great job she's doing as a mom. I'll urge her to accept the grace Jesus gives because missing the mark is part of being human. Motherhood is messy and nobody gets it right all the time. So why do I hold myself to a different standard? I can be gentle and encouraging to a friend, yet I strangle myself with an impossible expectation. Do you do this? Why do we do this?

For me, the answer is another shackling p-word—a close (and annoying) relative to perfectionism: pride. It is my pride that makes me want to hurry up and get over the struggle. I want to be able to say that I've checked off the mommy anger box with a definitive red X. Finished. Done. Never to be seen on the areas-of-required-growth-and-refinement list again! I don't want to admit to myself, to God, to anyone, that though I have made substantial progress in this area of boiling temper and better responses, I'm still far from perfect. I'm in process. You too?

On my own, I'm broken and inadequate. It's painful. But I'm also starting to see that it's kind of beautiful too. Jesus says, "My grace is sufficient for you, for my power is made perfect in weakness" (2 Corinthians 12:9).

I don't want to miss opportunities like I did today to teach my kids kindness, empathy, and more effective modes of communication. Though I botched the teachable moment for them, I didn't miss out on one for me. In this singing-versus-silence brother debacle, I learned (again) that I need Jesus.

Every moment of every day, I need Him.

I will always be inadequate in my own strength. Thankfully I'm not asked to parent (or work or be a friend or clean the house) in my own strength.

Neither are you, friend. Neither are you.

. . . .

one simple step

Choose one to practice today.

☐ Reach out to a friend and let her know you're struggling with anger. Ask if she is too. Commit to praying for each other.

☐ Choose one of the verses mentioned in this chapter and write it on a note card (Proverbs 15:1; James 1:19–20; Galatians 5:22–23). Put it somewhere you'll see it and read it often.

☐ Practice modeling a sincere apology and asking your child for forgiveness when you mess up. Try the simple phrases suggested: *I'm sorry for yelling. I should have used calm words. Will you forgive me?*

. . . .

one powerful prayer

Make this your daily prayer.

Jesus, thank You that You don't expect me to be perfect. Thank You that You love me even when I painfully miss the mark. Help me grow in self-control and dependence on You when I'm tempted to lose it. Amen.

seven

You Can Do This.
You Are Doing This.

Being a mom can feel like living in a foreign country where everyone knows the language but you. It can feel like driving on autopilot and suddenly realizing you don't know how you got where you are or how to get where you're supposed to go. Motherhood can feel like showing up to an advanced college class and realizing mid-lecture that you didn't take the proper prerequisites and you're expected to know things you don't.

Where's the translator? The map? The CliffsNotes? How was I possibly supposed to be prepared for this?

Do you know the feeling? One of the most disorienting and discouraging parts of being a mom is feeling like you'll never master the learning curve of parenting your child.

Maybe your motherhood story is unfolding pretty close to the plotline you always imagined. Maybe, like me, you're living a life you never once dreamed. Either way, I've yet to meet a woman who hasn't been rocked by at least one aspect of who her kid is and what it looks like to be their mom.

If you've ever had the thought, *I just can't do this*, let me stop right here and tell you clearly: You can do this. You ARE doing this! I can't give you an operating manual for your specific child. (Wouldn't that be an amazing thing to have!) But I can help you see more clearly that God has been writing your story all along and leading you to this moment. He has given you experiences to equip you and people to reflect back to you the good motherhood work you are doing, even when you can't see it.

Let me show you what I mean.

———

When I was seven, my best friend was a boy named Jack. He lived up a winding road on a hill that felt like a mountain. My mom knew the pass code for the huge black gate. When the wrought iron swung open, my heart swung free. I kissed her cheek and promised to be good, then leaped from the car to my waiting friend.

We waved to Jack's mom at the top of the driveway, signaling our consent to play by the rules. Then off we ran. Me and Jack. We crossed the sprawling lawn to the edge of the earth where rusty bottle caps became precious treasures and rocks must be ancient arrowheads.

Our next adventure was the dune. I can't fathom the purpose of such a massive pile of dirt other than the sheer pleasure of wild children. Brown clouds puffed around our feet as we scampered up the loose mound. Then down we slid, whooping and hollering in rowdy delight. We conquered the slope again and again until our pockets were heavy with dirt and my pale skin was plastered with enough dust to make me look like my tan-skinned best bud.

But my most favorite thing was the climbing tree.

Up that tree I was no longer a little girl with scraggly hair and a gap in her front teeth. I was strong and brave. I scaled fearlessly up the white bark, grasping each smooth branch as the tree swayed with the wind and our weight. Higher and higher we climbed— unrestrained, carefree. Finding a sturdy bough, we stopped to swing, toes dangling in the breeze. Then the race was back on to see who'd get to the tippy-top first. Up where the branches were more like twigs, we'd somehow perch together. Catch our breath. Let the wind carry our laughter.

Eventually, my mom returned. She spotted us near the clouds and started calling, "Be careful!" and "Get down now!"

Feet back on the ground, Jack and I listened to the appropriate reprimand about how we were far too high and quite unsafe. Yet the scolding was worth it. Every time. Because even if the height and freedom were temporary, I knew my heart was made to fly. I wasn't content to play with dolls and toy dishes. I was a climber. A seeker. A risk-taker and boundary-tester. I was independent, determined, often stubborn, and always full of spunk.

The Gift of Hindsight

I hadn't thought about Jack and our adventures in at least two decades. Then, one morning a few years ago, the memory came rushing back.

I peered out the kitchen window and saw my five-year-old barefoot in the backyard, digging in the spot we'd told him not to dig. It wasn't even 8 a.m. I opened the back door to call Elias in, but as soon as he saw me his eyes lit up.

"Mommy, Mommy! I found this *huge* buried stone and I think there might be *gold* underneath it!"

I heard the excitement in his voice. Smelled the crisp invitation of earth alive with dew. I saw the dirt crusted on his knees and wedged between his toes. And all my treasure-hunting, dirt-sliding, tree-climbing days with Jack came back in clear view.

The intended rebuke caught shallow in my throat—I knew my son just needed to be free. I breathed.

"Yes, buddy, I think you're right. I think there *is* gold under there."

He kept digging, and I went inside seeing the riches just unearthed.

You see, there is a richness to our stories. Hidden treasures of wisdom and insight that come with the gift of hindsight. There are story threads that may seem inconsequential at the time, like a little girl's love of climbing trees. But when examined from a broader perspective, that tiny thread becomes part of a grander strand.

Watching my boy crouch happily in the dirt, I was awestruck by the beauty of how God has woven my story together.

Many times since becoming a mom, I have wondered why God gave me three boys. Not that I wasn't thankful, not that I didn't love and cherish my all-male crew. It was just a different cast of characters than I'd pictured. It was a story I didn't feel prepared for. I grew up with mostly my mom and two older sisters. In a house full of girls, my tomboy days were short-lived. I knew more about Clinique compacts and pink-wrapped Tampax than I did about weapon noises and bathroom humor.

I loved my sons fiercely, but some days I felt surprisingly desperate in their presence. How do I thrive in a house full of boys who shout and wrestle till they laugh or cry? Boys with no volume control who make me feel out of control. Boys whose deep-down wild I cannot tame.

I had forgotten me and Jack. I had forgotten what it feels like to fearlessly crave the heights. Forgotten the deep need to live bravely beyond boundaries.

This window to my past was the way to remembering.

Now I can see the beauty of an out-of-the-box little girl whom God was preparing to one day become a mama. A mama who would need to understand that children thrive in freedom. Freedom to discover how God made the world and that each person in it is different.

I'm bowled over with wonder at the grace of His handiwork.

I hear a lot these days about the power of stories—how we need each other's stories. I wholeheartedly agree. But sometimes we need our own story. We need to look back and remember where we've been to understand where we are now.

Consider the parenting challenges you face today. Think about the thing that makes you feel out of your mom element. Now let your mind wind back through time. Is there an experience you've had before that connects to what you're experiencing now? Can you see how God might have used an earlier chapter in your story to prepare you for what you're currently living through?

Over the years I've wrestled with being a mom of all boys, in part because of the longing I felt for a little girl with bouncy pigtails. I felt a sense of loss for the pictures in my mind that would never play out in my life. Tiny strawberry-print swimsuits and saltwater sandals. Sharing a love for Judy Blume books. Watching my husband get dressed up for a father-daughter dance. I expected elaborate front-porch performances like my sisters and I put on with friends, complete with costumes, choreography, and scripted narration. I imagined cuddling by the fire watching *The Sound of Music* and *Little Women*.

But more than my unmet expectation of being the mother to at least one daughter, I questioned God's purpose in giving me the children He did because I lacked confidence that I had what it took to parent the kids entrusted to my care. I worried these boys would be better suited for someone else.

I'm sure there are ten thousand things I don't know about raising girls. I'm sure it's delightful and hard with its own brand of unexpected beauty and struggles. I'm also sure that if you're a mom of boys, there are countless ways our kids are different and my motherhood experience doesn't mirror yours.

But, for real. I've just got to tell you that *my* boys have introduced me to a version of childhood and motherhood I never once imagined. My boys are loud. Tactile. Physical. They are strong and smart and spirited. They are kind and creative and highly curious. All three are unique and different. But there is this part of them that I can only describe as boy-ness. Learning to understand it has felt like trying to understand a secret code I don't have the key for.

When Elias was born, my mom gave Noah a boy doll so he could have his own baby to take care of. This seemed like a good idea, a sweet gesture. Surely I had seen my friend's little girl happily pretend to burp her doll and change its diaper in tandem with her mommy taking care of the real baby. It wasn't quite the same scene with Noah. My nineteen-month-old promptly took that cute little baby, stripped off its blue overalls, tapped on its anatomically correct male part, then held it by the ankles, and with the full body swing of a professional golfer, he used that plastic baby head like a fairway driver and whacked a small rubber ball across the living room. His toddler arms shot up in victory as the orange ball landed in a basket of laundry.

There are just no words.

I remember another time playing in the boys' room as a family, building towers, looking at books, when Chris picked up a foam ball and threw it right at our son's head. Noah burst into laughter. Chris did it again and got the same hysterical result. Each time Noah laughed and put his little fingers together in the sign for more. *More, Daddy, more!* He loved it.

Chris looked at me. My face must have given away my utter perplexity.

"What? He's having fun."

"Never in a million years would I have thought to pelt our toddler in the head with a ball."

Now Chris was the one laughing.

Of course, these sweet and silly moments aren't the ones that stir up my feelings of inadequacy. But they serve as an illustration for how baffling parenting can be. No matter how many kids you have, no matter if they share your coffee-brown eyes or strands of your DNA, whether they are boisterous or shy, natural talkers or introverted dreamers, whether they love glitter and unicorns or video games and fart machines, there are parts of your kids and parts of motherhood that will make you feel painfully out of your element. Yet, you were also made for it. That is the tension.

The Eyes of Compassion

So how do we live in and move through the tension of feeling like we're not cut out for our specific kids or our particular life while also believing that God did not make a mistake in making us the mother of our children?

Like my story with Jack suggests, we can look back at our own story and identify ways God has already equipped us.

On more than one occasion I've had the pit-in-my-stomach experience of suddenly not being able to find my kid. When we're at the park and Elias disappears, panic sets in quick. I call and call, examine every wood chip, look in every bathroom stall. Eventually I look up and spy him perched on the plastic roof at the top of the play structure. I want to cry with relief and yell with angry disbelief. But I temper my lecture when I remember my own innate desire to climb as a child.

When Noah is freaking out over an itchy tag or Jude refuses to wear his only pair of clean jeans because they don't feel right, I remember my four-year-old self who had serious qualms about bumps in her socks and got tummy aches from wearing tight clothing.

Last week one of my boys had an eruption of anger that burst forth seemingly from nowhere. In the heat of the scene, he was unreachable in his rage. As I left him to smolder in his room, I kept doing the next mom thing, as we do. I put away popcorn and bell peppers and cartons of milk from our recent Costco trip. As I stewed over how to make sense of this behavioral mess, a memory suddenly flashed in my mind: It was me as a young child—tiny but mighty—raging in my bedroom. I can't tell you the reason now, but I know I was so mad at the babysitter that I tore my mattress off its frame and dragged it across the room to use as a barricade so that poor teenager couldn't open the door.

The memory softened me. *Oh, I'm not so unlike him. I have been where he is now.* Compassion washed over my frustration.

139

Even when we're flustered or dumbfounded by our kids' behaviors, even when we don't totally understand their strengths
or struggles, we can choose to see our kids' growing up (and our
growing with them) through eyes of compassion.

We can be irked yet remain tender. We can feel lost but remain
soft—toward our kids and ourselves.

Another key way to navigate the tension between feeling lost in
our mothering and trusting that God is guiding the way is to listen
to the stories other people are telling. I learned the power of this
lesson one summer while helping at VBS.

When each of my sons was four, I volunteered to help with
their group for our church's summer vacation Bible school. I feel
the need to tell you that this was like service *to the Lord*. I love my
kids. If you and I were real-life friends, I would love your kids—
because I love you. But children as an indiscriminate demographic
of people just aren't my thing. (Don't judge me. This is why the
body of Christ is made up of many parts. Rocking other people's
babies and teaching a crowd of kids are just not *my part*.) I'll talk
to a group of women and encourage moms all day long with great
joy. But spending three hours herding fifty four-year-olds from the
puppet show, to snacks, to games, to crafts stretches my gifting
and comfort zone.

I share this so you can have a sense of how I might have felt
at the end of the blessed VBS week. We were just ten minutes
away from pickup when happy parents would come get their rosy-
cheeked, sticky-fingered children and ooh and ahh over their hand-
painted garden signs. One of the other adult leaders and I were
outside making sure each kid's craft was labeled with the correct
name when I heard a loud clatter from behind a nearby utility
shed. I peeked around the corner. It was Elias. *My* four-year-old.
He was stacking paint cans he found who-knows-where in a teetering tower.

"Elias, get out of there. That is not a place to play. Please go sit
and color with your friends."

Two minutes later the canopy we were standing under started to shake. One side collapsed. There was Elias.

"I just wanted to see what this button did."

"Eli, you need to stay with the other kids. Go make me a Play-Dough pizza. Now."

I rolled my eyes and my friend laughed.

Soon parents came to check out their kids. VBS pickup can be a blur of commotion connecting the right kids with the right adults. Name tag, check! Parent signature, check! *Logan needs his craft. Lilly's mom is here—can a runner please call her from the indoor play area? Yes, Tyler had his gluten-free snack.* Focused, efficient, and personable were my goals.

Then, an ear-piercing scraping overtook my senses. I looked over my shoulder. There was Elias, again. Dragging a stack of metal folding chairs across the concrete.

Oblivious to my dagger eyes, Elias beamed, "Look, Mommy! I'm helping!"

When all the kids were gone, we finished cleaning up. Picking wads of Play-Dough out of the grass, I lamented to my friend Trisha how I wished Elias could just follow directions like the other kids.

She looked me in the eye and said, "Becky, he's a leader! Look how determined he is. He doesn't go along with everyone else because he has his own ideas. That's a fantastic quality. That little boy is going to grow up to do amazing things."

In moments like these, it's easy to laugh off the words of another person. It's easy to nod along while letting the encouragement, the insight, the truth, roll off your shoulders because your mind is busy rehearsing the script it's used to. This is what I was tempted to do.

I was tempted to say, *Oh, he's determined all right,* with a knowing wink while letting my frustration over his determined spirit remain. But what would happen if I let Trisha's unbiased observations of my son sink in? What if I let someone else's perspective help color the way I see my own child?

Because, really, the root of my frustration in moments like that with Elias isn't the fact that he's playing with paint cans and dragging chairs; it's the underlying fear that I'm not doing a good enough job. The spiral of inadequacy sounds like this in my head:

If I was a better mom, my son would listen.

If I could control him, things would go smoother and we all would be happier.

If I was a better disciplinarian, coach, or encourager, I would be able to channel his inner drive into expressions of compliance.

In short, my confidence hinged on his behavior. And that, my friend, is a broken ladder I'll never be able to climb.

I accepted Trisha's words as the gift they were. "You're right," I said, and let a smile spread across my face. "If this is how he is at four, I can't wait to see what kind of leader Elias is going to be when he's older. Surely God is going to use him for something special!"

God wants to build our parenting confidence by helping us see the goodness and beauty in our kids and in ourselves. He often uses other people to do it. Our job is to receive it.

Highs and Lows

This summer I had to go out of town for work during one of my husband's busiest weeks of the year. My trip was being planned last minute, and the typical people like grandparents who would normally step in and help weren't available. I ended up asking a local college student to help with our child-care needs. Karina knew the boys from church activities, but she had never babysat for us. Now, while I was on the other side of the country, she was going to take care of my kids for twelve hours—two days in a row. This was coming on the heels of two back-to-back family trips, and everyone was feeling the ache of being out of routine.

I left Karina a long list of instructions and ideas to pass the time. (With my silent prayer tucked in there. *Jesus, please let this go well.*)

Three days later, as I waited at the airport to return home, my phone lit up with a text from Karina:

> Thanks so much for having me watch the boys these past two days! You guys must be incredible parents to have raised three incredibly caring and independent boys. It was a pleasure spending time with them!

I read the message at least three times. Not because I was shocked by the great report—my boys really are fantastic kids who are maturing every year—but because I wanted the gift of encouragement to sink in. Deep.

Lord knew I would need it the next day when the aftermath of mustering up all their good behavior for someone else would unfurl. They seem to save all their back-talking, bickering, and emotional meltdowns for no one other than *moi*, me, their mama. I'm guessing you can relate.

This doesn't mean the babysitter or our kid's teacher would do a better job in our shoes. This means we need to listen closely and receive the sincere praise of others.

As moms, we get the joy of the highest highs and the pain of the lowest lows. No one gets hugs and kisses and whispered secrets like a mother. And perhaps no one hears "I hate you" and "You're the meanest ever" more than a mom. A child's tenderness and tantrums, affection and aggression, know no better home than the heart of a mom. This is what makes motherhood so beautiful and so brutal. This is what can shake our confidence.

Some women feel specifically called to motherhood. Others I know feel more like they stumbled or fell hard into it. Either way, I think we can agree that once you are a mom, we are called to steward the gift and responsibility well. But I used to think that if God called me to something, then I should be ready and able to do it—fully, completely, independently. The Bible paints a different picture.

I think about how Moses was called to lead the people of Israel, but he needed two friends to help hold his arms up. You can read the story in Exodus 17. Now, did Moses' tired arms mean he wasn't cut out for the job to which he was called? No. His weakness, his fatigue, wasn't a sign of his inadequacy; it was an opportunity to lean on the support of others. The fact that Moses needed Aaron and Hur to support his hands while Joshua went down to fight the battle was not a negative reflection on Moses. It was the lived-out picture of God's plan for us to need each other.

There will be things in life that we simply can't do alone—and we weren't meant to. Motherhood is one of them.

Words of affirmation about you or your child are like hands girding you up on either side. A friend's perspective is like borrowed strength to help you keep on keeping on in the work of motherhood to which you were called.

October, 2015, was a rough month. Noah was in the first grade and trying hard to meet expectations at school, only to unleash his pent-up stress on me later in the day. Elias was learning to mold into the new routines of kindergarten and having regular meltdowns at home. Jude was three. Sweet, compliant, and happy—until nap time came and his world spiraled into a tired, defiant debacle. This was also my first semester of graduate school. Years later I can point to all the ways we were experiencing growing pains, and it all seems normal and understandable. But in the thick of it I just felt desperately inadequate.

Was I wrong to start grad school when my kids were still young? Should I quit my part-time job and hope we had enough money to scrape by? Should I pull my kids out of school and educate them at home? Or just pull my hair out and crawl into a hole? These were the questions that swirled in my mind at 2:30 in the afternoon when emotions were high and my whole crew was falling apart.

144

In times like these, I hid in the laundry room and texted my friends.

> Pray now! The Keife ship is sinking in the tumultuous sea of proper letter formation and learning to read. I'm ready to resign from my post as captain. Let the crew fend for themselves. Jesus, save us!

Okay, my texts probably weren't that poetic. They were more like,

> One kid is wailing in his bed. Another kid is testing every boundary. And I'm losing my ever lovin' mind with the third one's back-talking. I don't know what I'm doing. Pray for me?

SOS prayer texts can be like a life raft—they buoy our hope and perspective.

After one of these texts, my friend Mindy quickly typed back that she was stopping to pray for me. As a mom of kids the same age, she got it. Then she added, "You are a wonderful mother. There is not a time we are together when I don't see you do something or say something and think, 'Oh, I want to do that/say that/be like that.'"

Years later I can quote this text because I saved it. I saved it so I could reread it whenever I needed it. Because here's the thing, friend: We can rarely see the full scope of how well we're actually parenting. All our feelings are intertwined with the big emotions of our children. We need other people to help us untangle our perspective. We need friends to help us see with fresh eyes and renewed hope that we really are the right mom for our kids, even when we feel at the end of our rope.

I don't think it was a coincidence that Mindy sent that specific encouragement when she did. God saw me in my struggle, just like He sees you in yours. He delights in sending us reminders of His love and care. He wants to whisper assurance that He's proud of you and that the Holy Spirit is available to empower you exactly when you need it. We just have to train our eyes and ears to receive these reminders when they come.

Our confidence grows when we choose to believe these God-given encouragements deep in our souls.

That October also marked my two older boys' first season playing soccer. For one kid, this could be known as paying money to watch your child sit in the grass and pick dandelions, or the joy of disciplining in public when your child chooses to climb the fence instead of listening to his coach. Good times.

In between trying to encourage Elias to engage with the team and redirecting Jude from playing in the rosebushes, I enjoyed getting to know another mom named Katie. I don't remember why I texted Katie after one of those exciting soccer practices—I was probably trying to track down a lost shoe or sippy cup—but I do remember the surprising text she sent back:

> I'm continually impressed by what a sensitive mom you are . . . how you nurture and care for each one of your boys in different ways according to their needs. I know I've only seen a tiny bit, but hang in there . . . you are doing a great job being their mom.

Do you see what I mean?

God is lavish in His love. Katie didn't send that because she had to. She said it because it was true. Trust me, I didn't *feel* like a sensitive mom. I felt fragile and inadequate. I felt like for whatever good thing I did, my mothering mess-ups were tenfold. Katie is the one who seemed calm and collected. She was always ready with a kind word and apt reply for her crew of four little kids around the same ages as mine. Through the gift of Katie's affirmation, I was able to see that my inner frazzle wasn't an accurate reflection of my competency as a parent.

I am the right mom for Noah, Elias, and Jude. I'm not perfect. But I'm the best mom to nurture, understand, and guide them in their growing up. And my good, good Father in heaven is ready and able and so very willing to equip me for the journey.

He's there to affirm and encourage and equip you too.

Straight from God's Heart

If I hadn't saved those texts from Mindy and Katie, they would have been sweet words in the moment but quickly washed down the drain of the day like gritty bathwater. We must record confidence boosters when we receive them! Don't dismiss them. Let them sink in. Let them mark your heart. Don't dismiss encouragement as random niceties or people just being polite. Take them in for what they are—love and assurance straight from God's heart to yours. It's one of the many ways He says, *I see you! I made you for this. I am with you and you are doing it. There's no better mom for this job than you.*

Decide today to look for glimpses of how God is already using you in your child's life. Are there things you can improve on? Sure. I see lots of areas of my motherhood and personhood I can grow in. But you can't parent with confidence if you never get off the treadmill of be-different, do-better.

You can't wait to *feel* adequate. You have to believe and embrace that God made you the mom of your child on purpose. Despite how parenting today *feels*, you can have deep peace and assurance that God is with you. No matter what your present circumstances are, God is for you. He who began a good work in you *will* carry it on to completion (Philippians 1:6).

Certain days, months, even entire seasons of motherhood are tougher than others. Our confidence cannot rest on our outcomes. Our confidence must come from the one place that a toddler

You can't wait to feel adequate. You have to *believe* and *embrace* that God made you the mom of your child on purpose.

meltdown, diaper blowout, or missed curfew cannot shake: in God alone.

Anchor your heart to this: "But blessed is the one who trusts in the LORD, whose confidence is in him" (Jeremiah 17:7).

Despite the stories of frustration I've shared with you in this chapter, I look back on the little years with my boys with great fondness. Nothing can compare with wrapping a toddler in a towel warm from the dryer. The way they'd say, "I wuv you, brudder" to one another. How Jude would tuck his chin tight to his chest and peer under his shirt, sure that if he looked hard enough, he would see Jesus in his heart. Their full delight in playing leapfrog in the backyard or opening a new package of sidewalk chalk. The even breathing of a child asleep on my chest— those days really were the best.

But I also look back and ache for the physical exhaustion and emotional weariness of feeling like I was not cut out for motherhood, especially with my firstborn. Between the ages of eighteen months and four years old, Noah was the hardest.

A few years removed from the height of our struggle, my mom was over one afternoon. We sat on the back-porch step and chatted about work and family while the boys played tag and hunted for roly-polies. Out of the blue, my mom said something that changed the way I look at my mothering.

With wistful reflection, she said of my then seven-year-old, "Noah has grown and matured so much. You and Chris have really done a great job with him. I think a lot of other parents would have accidentally crushed a spirit like his with stricter boundaries and harsher discipline to get him to behave. But the patience and grace you have shown him have made all the difference."

In those exceptionally tough years, I did not feel like a good mom. I was pretty sure everyone else thought I was failing too. I was convinced that someone else would be so much better suited to be Noah's mom. But now I see and believe the truth in my own mom's observation. God wanted *me* to be the mother who helped guide and shape Noah through those early years—and He wanted to shape me through them too.

That strong-willed, high-energy, stubborn and spirited and nonstop-active little boy is now ten years old. I could weep for the remarkable ways he has matured. The kid I never thought would stay in bed without a fight now stays tucked in and sleeps in peace. The boy I never thought would follow directions or sit still for more than five minutes is now thriving in school. Noah still has spirited qualities baked into his emotional and physical DNA, but I've learned to see that my job as his mom isn't to change who he is but help him grow into who he is becoming.

Parenting is never a straight road. (Oh, how I wish it were!) From the time a child enters our life, be it through birth canal, wide incision, or the painful labor of adoption, the motherhood journey is winding and unpredictable. The bumps and curves, uphill climbs and downhill plummets at breakneck speeds can be enough to fracture our confidence. Maybe even completely break it.

If you're in one of those rocky stretches that feels never-ending, I want to tell you that it will get better. You may not see a difference tomorrow or next week. Two years from now it still may be hard. But the landscape of your motherhood *will* change.

The work you are doing today is making a difference. Your prayers for patience, wisdom, and plain grit to keep pushing through the next hour are heard. Your continuing labor to mother well the child entrusted to your care is not in vain. Your investment in your child's life makes all the difference. Even more true, God working in you and through you will make all the difference.

To help you believe it, think back on your own story to a time someone affirmed you in your mothering. Grab a scrap paper and write down that word of encouragement. Now tape it to the dashboard of your heart. Then buckle up next to God. You can trust Him on this wild ride.

At some point in your motherhood journey, the road will pass through a lush meadow or turn along a sunny shore. The beautiful view and easy drive may last for a moment, a day, or even a long, sweet season.

Exhale. Give thanks. Roll down the window and listen to the breeze.

I'm pretty sure you'll hear, *Well done, daughter. Well done, precious one. You're exactly the mom I meant you to be.*

. . . .

one simple step
Choose one to practice today.

☐ Think back to who you were as a kid. What did you love? What did you struggle with? Ask God to help you connect the dots between your younger self and your child. Identify a way to apply your past experience to your current parenting.

☐ Write down an affirmation or encouragement you've received about your child or your mothering. Stick it on your fridge or bathroom mirror. Read it and believe it.

☐ Look for an opportunity to reflect the good you see in another mom. Tell her the strengths you see in her child. Let your words be a lifeline of hope for a friend.

. . . .

one powerful prayer
Make this your daily prayer.

Jesus, thank You for being the author of my story. I believe You've prepared me for my specific child and that You will continue to equip me for this parenting journey. Help me to see how You are working, especially when motherhood feels so hard. Thank You for being with me. Amen.

eight

Perspective Check, Check.
Is This Heart On?

Nothing seems to disrupt my motherhood journey more than a derailed perspective. I can be chugging away like a pretty little mama steam train and then suddenly my engine stalls or I lose my caboose or I look back and all the cars I'm pulling are completely off the track. *What just happened?* One moment I'm moving forward and the next I'm . . . stuck.

From daily distractions and resurging anxiety to unmet expectations and overwhelming seasons, there are so many things that can cause us to lose steam.

If you're anything like me, left to yourself your perspective on life and motherhood can change directions faster than a flimsy kite on a windy day. Soaring one minute. Plummeting the next.

Perspective is a powerful thing.

I don't want to be a mom who is easily shaken. I don't want my shifting emotions and circumstances to easily steer me off course. So how do we stay steady in life's ordinary motherhood storms? First, we need to recognize the things that threaten the stability of our perspective. Then, we need to understand what we can cling to. (Hint: It all points back to the unshakable truth and presence of Jesus.)

Friend, if you often feel rattled or distracted, if you love your kids fiercely yet feel overwhelmed by the responsibilities, lean in here. I've identified four key things that can threaten our motherhood perspective, and in turn, four practical ways we can cling to the gift and grace of the God who walks with us.

1. When distractions threaten your perspective, cling to the wonder of being present.

We finish dinner and my oldest boy looks across the table into his daddy's eyes and pleads for another round of baseball. I glance up at the clock. These longer daylight days can be deceiving to a six-year-old who thinks there's endless to time to play.

"We'll go outside as a whole family and each boy will get three buckets of balls to hit," my husband says. "Sound good?"

Noah and Elias cheer, offer the quickest mumbled, "May I please be excused?" and cram on their matching black Nikes with lightning speed. I take Jude out of his high chair, put a teetering tower of plates and forks in the sink, and return half-full sippy cups to the fridge.

I walk outside. The warmth of the day has burned off, replaced by a refreshing evening breeze. The sun is starting its daily descent. It shoots rays of glory through the neighbor's ancient oak tree.

"Mommy, let's sit together and watch brudders hit the ball!" my littlest shouts.

I pull two dusty step stools out of the garage and place them on the driveway out of Noah's deadly line-drive path. Jude sits on the white stool, then scoots the black one right next to his and pats the seat. I plop down on my appointed spot. The skin of our knees kisses.

Chris stands in the center of the grass coaching the kids through proper grip, stance, and swing. Elias glows with effort. Four years

154

old and smiling happy-sweet despite missing seventeen out of twenty balls. Noah shines with talent. Tennis balls soar over the roof. One gets lodged in the upper branches of a two-story tree. Six years old and swings like an all-star.

"Shag 'em up!" Daddy calls after the bucket is empty.

Jude launches from his perch next to me and joins the big boys chasing down balls scattered across the yard. I look to my left and see my favorite foxtails aglow with golden beams. I run inside to grab my phone. I frame up the gift with pixilated evidence. Fuzzy seeds clustered together like punctuation marks on tall grass. An ordinary landscape transformed by amber rays. Small glowing lanterns swaying in the breeze.

Chris teases that I already have a hundred pictures of this grass. Probably true. But there's no limit to the number of times you can breathe in beauty, stand in awe, or give thanks. Wonder is limitless. There is always more to capture.

I move to the middle of the lawn and click away as my boys hit away the evening light. They laugh and shout, "Did you see that, Mom?" as another ball rockets through the sky.

"Yes, I saw it!"

I see you, son, I whisper in my heart. *I see you.*

But I almost didn't.

On that night several years ago, I almost missed the gift of seeing. I had wanted to protest against my husband's request for the *whole* family to go outside. At the end of a meal I'm not thinking about having fun; I'm thinking about getting dishes done. Plates need to be rinsed and loaded. Pots scrubbed. Leftovers put away. Counters don't clean themselves, and the load of laundry with the blue school shirt Noah needs to wear in the morning won't leap into the dryer on its own accord. So if Daddy can occupy the boys outside with baseball, it's the perfect time for me to *get stuff done!*

After all, they don't *need* me, I reasoned. I have zero aim pitching, and I instinctively close my eyes whenever a ball is thrown my way.

Yes, there is always so much that needs to be done. But—I'm learning—there is always a great need to just be present. My boys may not need me to pitch or catch. But that doesn't mean they don't need me to watch. Cheer. Just be there.

Over the years I've written a lot about slowing down to see, savoring the moment, awakening to the wonder right in front of you. Maybe the message that thrums loudest in someone's heart is the one they need to be reminded of the most. Left to myself, I would have let productivity trump being present with my family. I would have let the perceived urgent blur my vision. But God knows I need some help, so He gave me a husband who reminds me (whether I always like it or not) to loosen my grip on my lists and embrace showing up in the moment.

Do you ever get all tightfisted and blurry-eyed too? Sometimes we need to step away from what feels most pressing so we can press in to what's most present. Sometimes we need to accept the invitation to be. To see.

Fixing my eyes on the small, immediate joys in front of me has been one of the most impactful ways I've learned to thrive as a mom. The decision to slow down and take notice is a powerful practice—closely linked to continuing to grow those deep roots of gratitude we talked about earlier. It shifts our perspective when we say, "This one moment I'm in, this one person I'm with, is of great value." And perspective is a powerful thing.

Our perspective can be the difference between joy and discontentment—the difference between apathy and engagement. A renewed perspective can take weariness or even bitterness and replace it with gratitude and purpose.

Every time I say yes to cheering on my kids as they hit tennis balls in the front yard, yes to noticing the beauty of sunshine and ornamental grass, yes to giving thanks for boyhood laughter and family time, it teaches my mama heart to soak in the simple gifts that make motherhood richest. The same is true for you. You experience the richness of motherhood when you savor the small moments that rushing on to the next must-do would make you miss.

There is so much at stake, friend. We can let moments get lost under the pedestal of productivity, or we can embrace opportunities to make memories with our kids and model what we value most: *them.*

What does your child most delight in? What lights the spark of joy in her eyes? What makes him feel like he's conquering the world? *Lean in there.* Even when it means surrendering your own pace or preference.

Learning to lean into small moments isn't a one-and-done kind of lesson. It's something we have to practice again and again.

Since Noah was a newborn, we have always enjoyed family walks. Whether with littles strapped in strollers for longer treks or toddlers scampering along as we stroll around the block, I'm a firm believer in fresh air and moving bodies.

Now, these little excursions weren't meant to be training for a speed-walking competition, but I also didn't want one loop around our cul-de-sac to take two hours! Yet that was a strong possibility when a kid wants to stop and look at *every single* rock, leaf, twig, and roly-poly.

Yes, that gray pebble is super-extra-special-magical, and it looks EXACTLY like the last seventeen you showed me!

Here's where the power of perspective comes in. In moments like this, we can choose to be irritated by the constant stops and interruptions, or we can embrace the opportunity to enter into our child's wonder.

Be quick to pause and marvel with them over that leaf shaped just like a heart. Lift your face to the sky and watch a hawk soar. Turn that smooth stone between your fingers. Talk about how it could have gotten so soft. Where did it come from? What adventures has that one rock been on? Pull out your phone and snap a picture of a caterpillar. Crouch down. Zoom in. Learn together to be awed over the beauty and intricacy of God's creativity. Sit on your front stoop or lie on the backyard grass and ask your daughter which cloud in the sky she likes best and why rainbows make her smile.

When we purpose to savor the small, the ordinary, we open our hearts up to greater joy and instill in our kids the power of a positive perspective.

Feel the silky satin of your daughter's ballet shoes. Tell your son how remarkable he is when he runs. Take a load of towels warm from the dryer and invite your littles to jump in the tickle pile. If your girl wants to twirl in the rain or watch the bathwater swirl down the drain, let the magic of the moment stretch a grin across your face.

Childhood isn't something to rush past, push through. The same can be said of motherhood. Their delight over snowflakes and dragonflies is our invitation to remember that watching them grow is a gift to be cherished.

Yes, there is so much to do as moms. I never imagined the weight of the never-ending tasks. I'm not trying to minimize or put a fuzzy filter on the legitimate work required in motherhood.

Blowing dandelion puffs and watching each seed take flight on a spring breeze won't change the fact that you still have to make dinner. Sinking your nose deep in the neighbor's yellow roses won't help your kid finish their math homework. I get it. But it will help you live with greater joy, promise, and purpose.

Consider the words of Psalm 9:1–2: "I'm thanking you, GOD, from a full heart, I'm writing the book on your wonders. I'm whistling, laughing, and jumping for joy; I'm singing your song, High God" (MSG). How would our motherhood change if we chose to let these characteristics mark our hearts and days?

I don't know a mom who doesn't want to live with a heart full of joy. We want motherhood to be fulfilling. We want our kids to grow up happy. We want to keep our eyes fixed on Jesus even when things around us are falling apart. We start by training to see the beauty and goodness of God in the ordinary pieces of our days.

When you're watching a family movie, lean over and count the freckles on your son's nose. Trace the curve of your daughter's ear with your finger. Notice the golden flecks in his irises. Call out the unique beauty in how God made your child. Pale eyebrows or mocha skin, wiry hair or dimpled cheeks, pause every day to get lost in the wonder of the one right in front of you.

2. When anxiety threatens your perspective, cling to prayer.

Last night I felt the familiar rise of anxiety. Tension crawling up the back up my neck. Mind racing. Hands slightly shaky. I couldn't catch a deep breath no matter how much air I filled my lungs with. I don't know if you've ever had this experience, but it's like coffee jitters in your heart even when there's zero caffeine pulsing through your veins.

My mind and spirit were overloaded by deep concern for people I love who are going through really hard things. Things like cancer and chronic illness and job loss and endless unknowns about what tomorrow holds. God gave me very tender wiring. I feel the shock and pain and heartache of others as if it were my own. From the middle of the night when I couldn't fall back asleep to all the in-between moments of my day, I had been praying for these dear ones. Claiming God's promises over them. Praising Him for the work He was doing and would yet do.

I was full of faith and hope, yet blanketed in sorrow. It can be both.

Now it was Tuesday evening. My night to write. Chris was taking care of dinner and then treating the boys to dollar ice-cream cones at our favorite local sweetshop. With wet hair and my favorite gray sweater, I was whirling around the house trying to get out the door and make the most of my precious time. Me. Computer. Panera. Stat.

159

I opened my laptop to eject the flash drive before slipping it into my tote bag, when I saw a new email. I clicked. My heart sank. Miscommunication? Misunderstanding? Had I missed the mark or had she? This was a situation without a clear resolution and I instantly felt miserable. My anxiety meter ratcheted up a few more notches.

I sat down to compose a response. My mind was a swirl of words and what-ifs, expectations and disappointments. And I still couldn't shake the underlying angst over my friends who were living big life-changing challenges that put my anxious heart and little work issue into proper diminutive perspective.

"Lord, I just can't write today," I whispered. "I just can't do the work."

Do you ever feel that way? Like life's crises and curveballs make the ordinary rhythm of your mom job, career job, your take-care-of-the-home-and-yourself-and-all-the-things job just too much? In that moment I wanted to close the blinds, get a big blanket, curl up on the couch, and watch a movie that would make me bawl. Sometimes that's exactly what we should do.

But this day, I needed to do the work God gave me. I needed to move through (not stuff down) my anxiety.

I needed to acknowledge my feelings, my frustrations, and the weight pressing me from all sides—and then promptly hand it all over to God.

I hit send on the email I had rewritten three times, put my laptop in my bag, and walked over to my couch. I kneeled down. And I poured it all out to the One who holds it all anyway. I named the friends whom I was hurting for. I prayed for the frustrating email, prayed for grace for me and grace for the other person.

In the midst of my praying I realized my hands were clenched in tight fists. So I made my physical posture a representation of my spiritual surrender.

Fists closed: *These things are not mine to hold.*

Hands open: *I surrender the outcomes to You.*

Fists closed: *These hurts are not mine to control.*

Hands open: *You are loving and good, and I entrust it all to You, Lord.*

I breathed in with each clenched fist and out with each open palm. It was helpful that I didn't have children running around, tapping on my shoulder, or asking for a snack. But I have done this kind of breath-prayer in a car full of noisy kids and while hiding in the laundry room.

Breathe in, breathe out. Breathe in, breathe out. A rhythmic re-hearsing of God's truth. Inhaling His promises. Exhaling my trust.

My knees started to ache. An injury from high school paired with being thirty-seven is rough. But with the stiffness of my joints came a lightness to my heart. God was with me. He would equip me for the one next thing I needed to do.

The day-to-day grind of mothering is full of challenges. I don't have to preach that message to you. You know it. You've lived it. You're living the mundane drain today. You're laughing over Eskimo kisses and tickle wars with your littles one minute, and cringing over another diaper explosion or back-talking tantrum the next. You're clapping loudly on the soccer sidelines or in the dance recital crowd, while cutting coupons and calculating how to stay out of the red. Whether you spend the fullness of your days with your kids by your side or you divide your time between work outside the home, your heart and mind are constantly pulled between places of celebration and frustration, delight and discouragement. Do you feel weary from the tension?

On my motherhood journey these past ten years, the tug-o'-war between joy and sorrow has been most difficult to navigate when kept in the darkness of isolation. There is an enemy of our souls who is like a prowling lion. He's hiding around the shadowy corners of our circumstances and emotions. He's ready to pounce, ready to steal, kill, and destroy anything with God's good fingerprints on it.

The thing this enemy has roared at my soul and hissed in my ear more than anything else sounds something like this: *You are*

161

the only one who feels this way. There is something wrong with you. You gotta do better, try harder. Don't be a failure.

Have you ever internalized a similar accusation?

At the heart of it is Satan's attempt to manipulate us into misplaced hope. He wants us to put our hope in ourselves. He wants us to rely on our own ability to hold it all together. That is not what the Bible teaches. "May the God of hope fill you with all joy and peace as you trust in him, so that you may overflow with hope by the power of the Holy Spirit" (Romans 15:13).

God is hope. He is our only true, lasting, secure source of hope. We were designed to place our trust in Him alone. I believe it with my whole heart. But I'll be honest, the biblical truth isn't easy to live out when life is just plain grueling or heartbreaking.

When hope feels worn and weary, fraying at the edges like a well-used security blanket, it's normal to wonder if there will be anything left to hold on to with all these unraveling threads. Before becoming a mom, I didn't know how easy it was to lose hope and how desperately I needed it. But what the enemy sets out to rob, Christ sets out to restore.

Jesus says it clearly: "The thief comes only to steal and kill and destroy; I have come that they may have life, and have it to the full" (John 10:10).

There are no promises that I won't continue to wrestle with anxiety. We can't control other people's behavior, reactions, or emotions. There are no guarantees against cancer and job loss and learning disabilities. "In this world you will have trouble," Jesus said. Yep. Check. So what do we do now?

We listen to what He said next. "In this world you will have trouble. *But take heart!* I have overcome the world" (John 16:33, emphasis mine).

Whatever is threatening your perspective today, find your sure footing in Jesus. Cling to prayer. Pour it all out to Jesus. Let Him hold it with you. Our troubles are not too big for the Overcomer. That's why Jesus came. Take heart, friend! He is near.

3. When unmet expectations threaten your perspective, cling to the good of what is.

Sometimes there's another unwieldy force from within that threatens both our perspective and our God-confidence; I'm talking about self-imposed expectations. I had to face this beast head on a few Augusts ago when my kids were six, five, and three.

The long of summer had melted fast like a bright-red Popsicle abandoned in the sun. In seven days my boys would start back at school. I felt like I failed summer.

I was about to launch the second-born piece of my heart and could hardly believe that in one short week I'd turn the corner from mom-home-with-lots-of-littles to mom-of-school-age-kids, and the bulk of my days would be spent with just my Jude.

This summer closing a hallmark motherhood season was supposed to be Hallmark perfect. The movie reels played in my mind with a Celtic/Taylor Swift/Jack Johnson soundtrack. (I have a vibrant imagination of what an outdoorsy/fun/laid-back summer ought to sound like.) The scenes flashed with cinematic flair from boys curled in cozy library nooks poring over books to new swimmers stroking long and confidently across a glimmering pool. I pictured productive mornings at the dining room table practicing letters, followed by happy park playdates reconnecting with old friends.

I say "Hallmark perfect" in jest because if you know me at all by now, you know I'm actually all about the real, gritty mess of life and motherhood, which is always full of beauty but rarely picturesque.

At the time I honestly didn't think my hopes were too lofty or my expectations too high. But nothing on my summer to-do list got done. My kids did not learn how to swim. They did not complete a summer reading program at the library. (Okay, for the sake of full disclosure, I'll go the distance and confess that we did not even step foot in a library. Not. One. Time.) We did not work on proper letter formation or reinforce the reading skills my oldest learned in kindergarten the previous year.

I don't recall deep cleaning a single thing, and that big basket full of who-knows-what on the side of my bed was not properly dealt with but rather strategically shifted week after week so as not to be tripped over or viewed when company came to visit. And there's a long list of friends I genuinely wanted to connect with, to share hearts with over iced coffee while watching tiny tanned bodies flail through backyard sprinklers—but good intentions fell short without timely initiation.

As I looked back on those fast-flying summer months, I saw the glare of not enough learning, cleaning, connecting, or reading, and too much glowing TV, blasting AC, yelling, rebelling, and close-quarter dwelling. The reflection made me feel pretty much defeated. Our whole summer disintegrated like that sad red Popsicle. Wasted away before fulfilling its full potential.

But before I drowned in a sticky pool of red-dye self-pity, I remembered the power of perspective. I opened my journal and read through hundreds of God-gifts scribbled down as thanks. I scrolled through my camera roll and saw countless moments meaningful enough to capture in pixels.

I remembered this: Focusing on my shortcomings crowds out memories of all the blessings.

And oh, there were so many blessings. Not fancy or expensive. Simple blessings so ordinary I almost forgot. Like painting rocks.

One glorious morning my three little explorers set out on a backyard expedition to uncover earthen treasures. We set up a washing station to carefully clean their stone discoveries. Once the rocks were baked dry by the summer sun, we laid paper grocery sacks over cracked concrete—high-tech painting stations. Budding artists in Superman pajamas were giddy to create. Forgotten moments now remembered. Savored. Wouldn't dare to trade.

I kept on memory-and-photo scrolling, determined to recall what other buried blessings made up our summer days and nights. *Soon the memories came streaming back.* . . .

- Lego-building extravaganzas that covered the dining room table for days. Imaginations soaring free and wild. Plastic masterpieces zooming through space, shooting galactic bad guys. Blessing.
- Back-porch dinners, all five of us crowding around one tiny bistro table. Watermelon juice dripping from lips. Blessing.
- Evening walks instead of early bedtimes. A soft summer breeze wrapping the sweet scent of star jasmine around sun-kissed shoulders. Childhood treasures of rubber bands and bottle caps discovered at every turn. Blessing.
- Summer storms breaking through the heat. Little ones catching raindrops on outstretched tongues. Digging race-tracks in freshly made mud. Watching the parched land drink in the unexpected blessing.

And how did I discount our first family tent-camping adventure? S'mores around a crackling fire. Hunting for lizards with Daddy's handmade grass lassos. Looking up at star-filled skies and crouching down to examine every pinecone. God's fingerprints at every turn. Blessings abound.

Sure, we were massacred by mosquitoes, two kids got bloody noses, and the other one puked on the winding road home. But the trip was not a failure. Not by a long shot. Could I dare say the same thing about that summer?

Dare I not forget the gazillion grains of sand molded into castles, the 487 rounds of Candy Land played, and ninety-eight hours of VBS songs sung. Dare I not minimize the countless stories read, a mommy and three children crowded on one bed. Or family movie nights and French toast dinners. Brothers battling in bedroom soccer (stuffed penguin as the ball), daddy-ref with the scoreboard app teaching sons how to be good losers and winners.

Could I have done summer better? Absolutely. But if I were reading this recap on your Instagram feed or listening to you retell the story in a coffee shop corner, I would never say *you* failed. I would say you showed up, lived real, loved well, did your best or at least good enough. And that is good. That is enough.

So I decided to muster the courage to whisper the same words to myself, both then and today. I've resolved to take stock of each blessing. Count every gift. Not to convince myself that I measure up as a mom, but to remember that God was with us. In us. Remember that summer—*life*—doesn't come with a pass–fail grade. It isn't judged on a rubric of productivity or graded on a bell curve of comparison to all the Facebook Joneses.

Summer is a season. A time to break. To breathe. To let children jump like ninjas through backyard sprinklers. And that's exactly what we did.

Isn't all of motherhood a collection of precious seasons strung together like Fruit Loops on a cereal necklace? The baby years and toddler years, the elementary school years and middle school years, watching our kids grow into teens and amazing young adults—these are all fleeting seasons. Let's not let the weight of self-imposed expectations crush the joy of each one.

If you feel like you failed at _____ [fill in the blank], do yourself a favor and take a few minutes to scroll your phone pics or stroll down memory lane and *remember*. Remember the good of what you did do. Shine a light on the moments with your kids that you don't want to forget. Softball season might have felt like a bust when you forgot the team snacks and your kid kept striking out, but remember that one fly ball she caught and the way you cheered till your throat was raw.

Big or small, let the triumphs ignite a spark of gratitude. I don't know what thing from the past is threatening to derail your parenting confidence and present perspective, but I know looking for and celebrating the good is a powerful antidote for unmet expectations.

4. When overwhelm threatens your perspective, cling to truth.

Sometimes the present moment is truly overwhelming. Some days you can't put off the tasks or press pause on the responsibilities to photograph grass or paint rocks or count freckles. (Most of those marks are probably dirt anyway because *somebody* refuses to bathe.) Some days your perspective is dark and desperate because that's an honest reflection of the load you're carrying. I get it.

There was a night not so long ago where the only thing I could see in front of me was a long road of barriers. The way forward seemed impassible.

My husband was delayed more than an hour, and my patience with the kids was shot. Their whining and bickering was only matched by my exhausted irritation. There was nothing catastrophic happening, just the pressure of regular life building under a tight lid. I needed to let some steam escape before I blew it.

I was waiting at the front door when Chris walked in. Before the poor guy had a chance to set down his bag, I told him the kids were fed, teeth brushed, and I needed to take a walk around the block. *Love you. Thank you. Good-bye.*

Ugh. I was just done. The kids were only part of it. I was in the middle of an intense semester of graduate school and had recently taken on more responsibilities at work. I had moved into a season of juggling motherhood and education and finally a job that I loved. These were gifts. They brought me great satisfaction and deserved my full investment. I wanted to give each my very best, but I felt like I was drowning in the bare minimum.

With dusky-gray sky overhead, I let the evening air fill my lungs. One foot in front of the other. Step, step. Step, step. Deep breath. The rhythm of my feet helped move my heart toward Jesus. I was ready to pour out my overwhelm to Him.

Even in letting my tangled emotions unravel before the Lord, I still felt knotted up. Stuck.

167

This wasn't a matter of simply confessing my stress, identifying something to cut back, and choosing a more lighthearted perspective. My predicament wasn't that I was just hormonally cranky or that I had taken on more than I should—though both of those things have been true *on several* occasions. This time I was emotionally steady doing exactly what God had for me. My job was an unexpected gift straight from Him. Working toward my master's degree wasn't in my current plan, but the Lord had also swung that door wide open, and I knew I was in a season of being stretched for a reason. Yet I didn't want these things to replace the time and energy I devoted to my kids.

The sun was beginning to set, and I still felt like a mess.

I pulled out my phone to leave a voice message on Voxer for my friend Elise. I needed to process out loud the question banging on the walls of my heart. Elise has six children. Runs a ministry and business. If anyone would have an answer, it had to be her.

"What do you do when what you have to give is not enough for what is needed?" I pleaded into the phone.

Faced with commitments that I couldn't break, looming deadlines, and pressing practical needs (like dinner to eat and clean socks on feet), again I was in a place of "not enough." Not enough time. Not enough energy and clarity. A wavering resolve to keep on keeping on.

With a two-hour time difference between California and Texas and nine kids between us, it's typical that Elise and I will leave messages for one another and not be able to reply right away. But this time my friend was listening as I was spilling my weary heart, and she messaged me back immediately.

Her message could have said a lot of things. Elise could have complained about her own day. She could have commiserated with me and affirmed how right I was to feel overwhelmed. She could have compared my challenges to her own, which far outweighed the work-, school-, motherhood-heavy blessings I was carrying. Instead, she reminded me of the story of the five loaves and two fish. The story of when Jesus took what was not enough and made it more than enough.

I walked home as the sky glowed orange behind me.

The next morning, I woke up feeling like I was already drowning. Before my day even began, I felt doomed to defeat. Do you ever feel that way?

I got the kids off to school and couldn't shake what Elise had said. "God can make your not enough into more than enough."

I was familiar with the loaves-and-fishes Bible story. Jesus took a meager meal and fed five thousand people. Got it. Check. As a kid I had seen it played out on plenty of Sunday school flannelgraphs. But I didn't see its immediate relevance to my situation. Apparently I needed to learn it again.

> As evening approached, the disciples came to him and said, "This is a remote place, and it's already getting late. Send the crowds away, so they can go to the villages and buy themselves some food." Jesus replied, "They do not need to go away. You give them something to eat." "We have here only five loaves of bread and two fish," they answered. "Bring them here to me," he said. And he directed the people to sit down on the grass. Taking the five loaves and the two fish and looking up to heaven, he gave thanks and broke the loaves. Then he gave them to the disciples, and the disciples gave them to the people. They all ate and were satisfied, and the disciples picked up twelve basketfuls of broken pieces that were left over.
>
> Matthew 14:15–20

Sitting at my kitchen desk that morning with a sink brimming with dishes behind me and piles of books and papers in front of me, it was like Jesus lifted my chin and said, *See Me. See how I can take a total lack and turn it into total satisfaction.*

Those five loaves and two fish leapt off the flannelgraph. This wasn't a dusty children's story. This was fresh promise for today.

As a kid I wasn't tuned in to the full context of this story. Maybe the surrounding details are fuzzy in your mind too. Let's briefly unpack the circumstances that led to this miracle-meal moment. Jesus and His disciples were in a remote location because they were trying to escape from the crowds. They needed a break from all their obligations. You see, John the Baptist—Jesus' cousin, friend, and forerunner in ministry—had been murdered. Beheaded. Jesus and His friends were understandably distraught. They needed space to breathe and grieve. But people followed them anyway. Now a huge crowd was pressed together up against a mountain. Daylight was fading, and if they didn't do something quickly, they would all be stranded there for the night without food.

No doubt Jesus and His disciples felt pressed from all sides. That's a feeling I can relate to. You too?

What struck me reading the story this time was what preceded the miracle of multiplication: *Jesus gave thanks.* Before there was enough food to pass around, before the problem was solved or their predicament averted, Jesus looked up to heaven and gave thanks for what was already provided. Could I do the same?

That story changed my perspective on that hard day. It's continuing to change all of my days as I allow God to reshape the way I think about my not-enough.

I've never had God give me an abundance of bread and fish, but I have seen Him multiply my time, energy, joy, and creativity more times than I can count.

I've got a hunch you could use a miracle or two in your week. Can I encourage you to let Scripture be your perspective-setter?

Instead of focusing on your lack, first give thanks for what you already have. Then look to God. Eyes up to heaven. Surrender your heart to His best for you.

Remember that hungry, desperate, stuck crowd and how Jesus must have felt. Trust that when trials come your way and things don't unfold the way you planned, your overwhelm is actually an opportunity to experience God's power.

Your overwhelm
is actually an
opportunity
to experience
God's power.

Let me say that again: Your overwhelm is an opportunity to experience God's power.

Your not-enough is an invitation to receive His more-than-enough.

Your inadequacy is a chance to be filled up with God-confidence.

I know it rarely feels like it, but our lack is a gift. *Jesus, help us to see and receive the gift!*

I got to the end of that stressful day, to the end of that intense work season, to the end of grad school the same way I'm getting through each day of motherhood—knowing with every fiber of my being that I did it by God's strength in me.

You, dear mama, can get through today's impossible by God's strength in *you*.

Pour out your tangled heart to Him.

Apart from Jesus, we've got nothing.

Get ready to receive His beautiful, unexpected something.

* *

one simple step

Choose one to practice today.

☐ Purposely set aside your desire to be productive and be fully present with your child. Let the joy of a small moment fill you with gratitude.

☐ Practice a simple breath prayer. Breathe in, *God, I'm feeling anxious today.* Breathe out, *I trust that You are with me.*

☐ Fill in the blank: I feel like I failed ____. Now take a minute to remember the good of what you did do. Celebrate the small blessings of what did happen.

☐ Identify an area of not-enough in your life. Thank God for what you already have and ask Him to multiply it. Then watch for the ways He transforms your lack today.

one powerful prayer

Make this your daily prayer.

Jesus, thank You that I don't have to stay stuck in my doubts or distractions. When I'm feeling unsteady, I can cling to You because You're right there walking with me. Help me to see You, to choose You, in the everyday moments of motherhood. Be the One who directs my perspective. Amen.

nine

The Thing You Really Need
More Than Caffeine and Sleep

I'll be honest. I mostly signed up for the free child care. I saw it advertised in the church bulletin—a Tuesday morning women's Bible study starting soon. The announcement had all the details for time, location, cost, curriculum, contact info, but it was these words that stopped my eyes in their skimming tracks: child care available for ages 0–5. I didn't know how I would complete the weekly material or get out of the house on time or if I would connect with the women, but the thought of having my three-year-old and two-year-old and three-month-old lovingly cared for *by someone else* for two hours every Tuesday was like winning the hope-for-my-soul lottery. I was in.

I showed up the first day with my Beth Moore *Mercy Triumphs* study book in one hand and an unexpected load of fears and insecurities in the other.

It had been so long since I did a serious Bible study. College maybe? *What if I can't keep up with the daily homework? What if I'm not spiritual enough or insightful enough or awake enough to do this?* I've always been a high achiever. I don't like to do things unless I can do them with excellence. (Needless to say, motherhood has helped unwind and tangle back up that part of my wiring.) My thoughts continued to swirl. *Did I pack enough diapers? Did I apply enough layers of concealer?*

The women's ministry director gave a warm welcome from the stage and explained how this particular study was set up a little differently. Normally, she would preassign women into small discussion groups. But Beth Moore designed *Mercy Triumphs* with four different commitment levels: from the basic level of just showing up and watching the group videos, to the highest level of doing the daily homework plus reading the in-depth articles plus memorizing the book of James on which the study was based. There was freedom to participate at whatever level worked for your life season. Too often women drop out or disengage because the time investment is more than they can give.

Bingo! I thought. If anyone was entitled to elect for the lowest commitment level, it was a mama with three kids under the age of four! I sighed with relief in my cushy seat.

But then the woman with the microphone reiterated what Beth had spoken in her introductory video. Along with full freedom to come as you are and do what you can, there was a challenge: Choose one level up from where you feel comfortable. Trust God to empower you and transform you by reaching outside your comfort zone for more of Him.

If you've ever experienced a sudden stirring by the Holy Spirit, you know what an uncomfortable, heart-pounding-in-your-throat experience it can be. I checked my phone to see if it was time to run over to the nursery to feed Jude. Nope.

"We'll be passing out green cards with the four different commitment levels. Please take a moment to quiet your spirit and hear from the Lord about which path He is leading you to take. Write your name and check the box that applies to you. Next week you'll receive your group assignment based on your selection."

I wanted to strain my neck to see what other people were checking. I wanted to ask the handful of women I knew scattered around the room which level they were choosing. But I closed my eyes. Willed myself not to nod off. And prayed, *God, I know that I'm here because I need more than just a break from my kids. I know I need more than extra sleep and hot coffee. Help me hear You. Show me what You want me to do.*

I grabbed a tiny yellow pencil from the chair-back pocket in front of me. Printed my name. Took a deep breath. Checked a box.

My Scary, Sacred Yes

Over the next week, one thought kept cycling through my mind like the load of towels I kept having to rewash. *What did I do? What did I do? What did I do?* The thought came in rhythmic waves while I burped the baby and filled up the gas tank and built another block tower for a toddler to whack down in crashing glory.

Regret? Fear? Hopeful expectation? I wasn't quite sure what the feeling was—but something big was stirring all the way from my gut to my heart to the spin-cycle of my weary mind. I had checked the box next to number four. The top level of Bible study participation and commitment.

Why in the world did I do that? I can't even go in Target and come out with the five items I went there to get! How on earth do I think I'm going to *memorize* the entire book of James? What had possessed me to commit to such a thing?

I had checked my heart about it more than a dozen times. Was I falling back into my performance mentality, thinking that I had to do more to earn the approval of others (maybe even the approval of God)? Did I choose it because I thought that was my best bet of being placed with my friends? Was this a last-ditch effort to do something that I could control when so much else in my life with three littles felt out of control? Maybe I should just eat the fifteen-buck book fee and not go at all. I mean, it's in the middle of the baby's morning nap, and dropping off Noah and Elias in child care is a crapshoot—no telling if they'll run into their class like it's a candy store or resist like enemy territory.

I was still chewing on my choice come Monday night. I wanted pure motives. I also wanted the path of least resistance. Maybe this season of motherhood wasn't the season for saying yes to something outside our routine. As the big boys splashed their lavender bath bubbles, I hoped the soothing scent would somehow calm my anxious spirit.

Later, as I wrangled three boys into three sizes of diapers and three sets of footie pajamas, I felt a wrangling in my heart. And I knew that in the same way I wanted my wiggly babies to just quiet down and let me give them what they needed, God wanted the same from me.

Becky, I have so much more for you than a couple of hours of free child care. I have the kind of break and breakthrough your heart really needs. I have more of Me. Will you let Me give you what you need?

I want to pause this story to address something that I've wondered when reading other books, and maybe you're wondering it now too. *Is God actually speaking to her?* I did not hear the audible voice of God. I believe it's possible, though it's never been my experience. But I have learned how to listen to His Spirit speaking to mine.

It's like Jesus explained to His closest friends, "But the Counselor, the Holy Spirit, whom the Father will send in my name, will teach you all things and remind you of everything I have told you" (John 14:26 CSB). This was Jesus' promise to His disciples before He was betrayed and crucified. Jesus' friends had gotten used to hearing His voice, following His lead, doing life side by side. After Jesus returned to heaven, the Holy Spirit was God's gift to those who believed in Him. If you have received the gift of salvation in Christ, then the Holy Spirit is yours too—your counselor, your advocate, your guide.

When a vivid thought or feeling or a strong urge to act rises in my mind, I take notice. I ask myself a few questions:

- Where did this feeling come from?
- Is this something I would normally think or say to myself?
- Could this be my internal projection from someone else? (As in, am I thinking the way so-and-so might think about this? Am I trying to please or perform for someone other than God?)
- Does this idea or action align with Scripture and God's character?

Here's an example of how this could play out: Say in my mind I heard something like, "You're too emotionally and physically exhausted. Signing up for an intense Bible study is just setting yourself up for failure. You're not going to be able to follow through. It's probably best to stay home and avoid disappointing yourself and your group." If this was the voice in my mind, I'd be tempted to agree. This thinking makes sense according to my circumstances and lines up with my feelings about the situation. But this sounds like *me*—at least part of me. It sounds like my fears and insecurities. But it does not sound like God's heart.

God's heart says, *I will strengthen you, provide for you, and empower you.* That's what He said to Paul when the apostle was desperate. "My grace is sufficient for you, for my power is made perfect in weakness." Despite feeling powerless to overcome the thorn in his flesh, the thing that made him feel limited and weak, Paul believed God. We see it in his response: "Therefore I will boast all the more gladly about my weaknesses, so that Christ's power may rest on me" (2 Corinthians 12:9).

Paul experienced the truth of God's promise. Five years later in a letter to the Colossians, he declared, "He is the one we proclaim, admonishing and teaching everyone with all wisdom, so that we

may present everyone fully mature in Christ. To this end I strenu-
ously contend *with all the energy Christ so powerfully works in me"*
(Colossians 1:28–29, emphasis mine).

If God had left Paul high and dry, if He had let Paul flounder in
his weakness, let that metaphorical thorn fester and get infected,
I don't think Paul would have kept trusting God and telling others about Him. But Paul did! Later in the same letter, the apostle
writes, "So then, just as you received Christ Jesus as Lord, continue
to live your lives in him, rooted and built up in him, strengthened
in the faith as you were taught, and overflowing with thankfulness"
(Colossians 2:6–7).

Back in my boys' room, wrestling their wiggly bodies into bedtime readiness, I knew what the Spirit was asking me to do. No,
not *do*. I knew what He was inviting me *to*. It had been a long time
since I had received Christ Jesus as my Lord—and to be honest, it
had been a long time since I had purposefully sought to be rooted
and built up in Him.

My faith felt weak. I felt empty. I longed for a filling up that
would last longer than the fleeting boost from a reheated cup of
coffee or twenty-minute power nap.

A Tuesday Morning Invitation

The next morning I showed up at Bible study ten minutes late with
no makeup, kids with crazy bedhead, and a baby demanding to be
fed. But I showed up. God didn't care whether I felt put together
or completely disheveled, whether I came feeling strong or weak;
He just wanted *me* so that He might give me more of Him.

Accepting God's Tuesday morning invitation turned into nine of
the most foundational months in my entire motherhood journey.

I share all this backstory because I want you to know that hope
and growth sometimes look like wrestling.

Even though I knew on that very first Tuesday that God was
asking me to say yes to being *all in* for this study, it took another

week, and another week after that, and probably a dozen more after that to believe and trust and grow in confidence that I really had heard from the Spirit. That He really did have something in His Word to say—to me.

My fear said investing my time and energy into studying and memorizing Scripture was going to leave me more depleted than I already was. Wrestling through that fear revealed a different truth: God's Word fills you up.

What I see now is that motherhood is a life season that highlights part of the long-standing human condition. We will be thirsty! On our own, we are designed to be empty!

Why the exclamation points, Becky? Being doomed to perpetual thirst and emptiness doesn't sound like a positive thing to me, you might be thinking. Trust me, this news is *good*—way better than a new episode of your favorite show or earning a free latte on your birthday.

My emptiness and inadequacy—your emptiness and inadequacy—isn't a poor reflection of our character or a judgment of our parenting. It's actually a gift. Like a flashing neon sign in your soul embedded by your Creator pointing to the true source of confidence and filling.

I came to understand that my nagging longing for something *more* in the midst of the fullness I already had had less to do with motherhood, my circumstances, or my personal capacity, and everything to do with my spiritual reality. Do you see the freedom in this distinction?

Sayonara, entangling guilt and shame! Adios, every lie that says I should be perfectly fulfilled by motherhood alone.

God expects us to be thirsty because He designed us to be quenched by His living water. People have been wrestling with this part of the human condition since long before moms were fretting over whether organic cotton diapers really make a difference or if their kids' dental health would be permanently damaged by drinking juice or failing to floss. Before there was the pull of social media and after-school activities, before there was the option of working inside the home or out, before there were libraries full of self-help books and hundreds of podcasts with expert parenting advice, before any of the dilemmas or opportunities or motherhood pressures we face today, there was a God who sees the needs of His people.

Listen in. Maybe these ancient words are exactly what your heart needs to hear today:

> "Hey there! All who are thirsty, come to the water!
> Are you penniless? Come anyway—buy and eat!
> Come, buy your drinks, buy wine and milk. Buy without money—everything's free!
> Why do you spend your money on junk food, your hard-earned cash on cotton candy?
> Listen to me, listen well: Eat only the best, fill yourself with only the finest.
> Pay attention, come close now, listen carefully to my life-giving, life-nourishing words.
> I'm making a lasting covenant commitment with you, the same that I made with David: sure, solid, enduring love."
>
> Isaiah 55:1–3 MSG

These words are for you, friend. God is speaking to you. *Come close. Be filled up with life-giving, life-nourishing words.*

In this world where so much is unsure and unstable, where so much of what is offered is just fleeting pleasure, God is offering sure, solid, enduring love.

I don't know if the lightbulbs are going off for you the way they are for me, but when I read this passage, I sense the Spirit's sweet assurance: *There's nothing wrong with you, Becky. Your thirst, your emptiness, your neediness, your wrestling and restlessness—it's not something for you to overcome. You don't have to get over it. These feelings are like arrows—pointing you to Me.*

Dear mama, in case you need to hear it, let me say it plainly: There is nothing wrong with you. If motherhood has unearthed a hidden vault of weakness and inadequacy, you are normal. If you love your children with all that you are but at times feel an emptiness you never could have imagined, consider yourself in good company. I'm right there with you. These dueling feelings aren't a condemnation—they're an invitation.

I find the continuing passage from Isaiah helpful.

Seek GOD while he's here to be found, pray to him while he's close at hand. Let the wicked abandon their way of life and the evil their way of thinking. Let them come back to GOD, who is merciful, come back to our God, who is lavish with forgiveness.

Isaiah 55:6–7 MSG

God is inviting you and me into deep, life-giving relationship with Him. When we seek Him, we will find Him. When we pray, He will listen. God isn't disappointed in your weakness. He's not disgusted when you mess up. He's not holding every poor choice, bad attitude, negative thought, or temper flare-up against you. God is tender toward you. Merciful. He *lavishes* forgiveness.

How can this be? I'm tempted to wonder. I often hold all my junk against me. Why wouldn't He? Let's keep reading.

"I don't think the way you think.
The way you work isn't the way I work."
GOD'S DECREE.
"For as the sky soars high above earth,
so the way I work surpasses the way you work,
and the way I think is beyond the way you think.
Just as rain and snow descend from the skies
and don't go back until they've watered the earth,
Doing their work of making things grow and blossom,
producing seed for farmers and food for the hungry,

183

So will the words that come out of my mouth
not come back empty-handed.
They'll do the work I sent them to do,
they'll complete the assignment I gave them."

Isaiah 55:8–11 MSG, emphasis mine

Friend, this is the promise I clung to seven years ago. This is the promise God came through on for me: *The Word of God does not return empty.*

I didn't know how saying yes to *all the things* for that Tuesday morning Bible study could possibly fill me up when I was pouring out from a depleted place. But God doesn't work the way I do. When He promises something, He does it—big time!

I discovered that God's Word wasn't meant to be an accessory or afterthought. Scripture wasn't something to make my life more palatable, like a fudgy brownie at the end of a long day. God's Word was meant to permeate everything—a permanent lens through which to see and understand life and all its moments big and small.

When I started reading James that September, it was easy at first to get bogged down in the language. If you haven't spent much time reading the Bible, the wording can initially feel foreign. Was this really accessible for an exhausted mom of three littles? But it didn't take long to see that, oh yes, this was most definitely for me.

Need to understand the purpose of trials? Need some extra wisdom? Struggle with anger or being judgmental? Want your faith to be more than the "right" answers and actually change your life and the lives of others? Raising my hand high. This was all packed into the book of James. This was what God had waiting for me.

Now, before you start thinking this means I magically escaped the fray of potty training, don't-eat-rocks reminding, and nipple-cream applying, let me tell you how this whole Bible study thing shook out. I worked on my study questions while Noah and Elias watched an extra episode of *Curious George* and the baby sat in his bouncy seat at my feet. I read one passage of Scripture while the boys ate snacks strapped in their high chairs. There were count-less interruptions. I'd get distracted and forget what I was reading or writing. I let it be imperfect. I left some sections half-done. I skipped portions of the in-depth articles. I did what I could and gave myself permission to let that be good. Let that be enough.

But the one thing I knew I needed to dig into, no matter what it took, was the part that felt the most impossible—my commitment to memorize Scripture.

Scripture and Small Victories

One of the gals in my Bible study group offered to laminate each chapter of James so each woman could have a sturdy copy to take anywhere. *Ahh, something that can't get ruined by projectile spit-up. Perfect.* That 8½ by 11 plastic sheet became like a third appendage. I took it to the doctor's office. I took it to the park. I read it while I cleaned the kitchen. (Which may or may not have caused me to put away a dishwasher full of *dirty* dishes.) I read it sitting on the grass while the boys made dragon forts in backyard planters. I read and memorized one verse at a time by the glow of the nightlight while I nursed the baby at midnight and 3:00 a.m. and 5:30.

Sometimes I could only hang on to a few words, a single phrase. Like the part from chapter two after which the Bible study was named. *Mercy triumphs over judgment.* Burp the baby. *Mercy triumphs.* Change his diaper. *Mercy triumphs.*

That was all I could do. And that was good. That was enough.

Slowly, slowly, those words and phrases strung together in verses and paragraphs. My weary mind that I thought couldn't hold one more thing was being held together by the Word of God. I started to crave it.

Right when I was at the very end of myself, God showed up.

He expanded time and used His Word as the lifeline I didn't know I desperately needed. During early morning couch cuddles with *Dinosaur Train* singing in the background, in the shower with toddlers splashing at my feet, while stirring splattering spaghetti with a baby on my hip, I memorized James. For nine months, in the crevices of my days, I repeated the words. Out loud to myself. In whispered prayers. In silent meditation, I repeated them. Again and again until they became etched in my mind—memorized.

God used His Word to fill the cracks in my heart.

I was most surprised by the way a verse suddenly came to mind exactly when I needed it. Not when I felt super religious. Not when I was having a good day and holding it all together by my own strength. I didn't think of it when I was at church or listening to worship music. Scripture came alive in my mind like it never had before in moments of desperation. Like an unseen rescue ship to a flailing swimmer.

On nights I sat in the hallway with my back against Noah's closed bedroom door, tears streaming down my face, listening to my four-year-old rage over bedtime. I was certain this situation, this child, was beyond reason—beyond the reach of Supernanny herself! This not-so-super mom (and dad) had tried everything. Tried and failed and tried and failed, and still on and on our strong-willed son wailed. Through the angst of a nightly routine that felt like a wide-awake nightmare on repeat rose the words from James 1:5: "If any of you lacks wisdom, you should ask God, who gives generously to all without finding fault, and it will be given to you."

When I didn't know what to say or do, God's Word became my fledgling prayer. With barely enough end-of-the-day, end-of-myself strength I whispered back to Him, *I need Your wisdom. I'm asking. Please heap it on. I don't know how to help my son. I don't know how to make this better. Help me. Reveal to me the way I cannot see.*

God's Word showed up on mornings like the one when I walked into the bathroom to find a child using my hairbrush like a toilet scrubber. Is it too much to ask to live without the constant need for disinfectant? As my blood pressure started to rise, so did James 1:19–20 in my mind: "Everyone should be quick to listen, slow to speak and slow to become angry, because human anger does not bring about the righteous life that God desires."* *Slow to become angry.*

"Noah, my hairbrush doesn't belong in the toilet."

"But I'm helping you clean, Mommy!"

"Thank you for wanting to help, buddy. Next time please ask me *how* you can clean. I will give you the right tool to use. Mommy doesn't like to brush her hair with pee water."

Deep breath. Small victory. Hug my son. Disinfect the brush.

I gave thanks for a perspective beyond my present circumstance. *Thank You, Jesus, for the power to override my natural reaction. Anger doesn't bring about the life I desire either.*

I could give you a dozen more examples from everyday mom life of how God used Scripture to strengthen my spirit and equip me.

He doesn't wait until we feel adequate. He doesn't wait for our insecurities or real insufficiencies to be resolved. God meets us and equips us when we're smack in the murky, magical middle of motherhood.

In many ways I felt like the Samaritan woman who met Jesus at the well. Day after day she came to that well to draw water that would quench her thirst. I imagine how weighed down she felt making the trek to the outskirts of the city. Not only by the heavy buckets she carried, but by the heavy burdens of her own sin, of the life that wasn't turning out the way she planned. Though Jesus asked her for a drink, He was actually there to address her deeper need. "Everyone who drinks this water will be thirsty again, but whoever drinks the water I give them will never thirst. Indeed, the water I give them will become in them a spring of water welling up to eternal life" (John 4:13–14). I needed the water Jesus was offering as much as the Samaritan woman did.

Four years into motherhood and I was painfully parched. I had lugged my bucket to the wells of afternoon naps, Netflix binges, and Facebook scrolling. I tried to satisfy my yearning with countless tubs

---

* My paraphrase.

of peanut butter frozen yogurt. They were temporary, numbing plea-sures. But nothing could permanently fill my deep place of need.

How tender God was to call me to Him through the gift of free child care.

In a season when I was barely trudging through the ashes, God used a Tuesday morning Bible study to spark a blazing fire in my heart for Him.

Are you in the ashes today, friend?

Are you tired of schlepping around your own leaky bucket? You don't have to keep trekking to a source that doesn't satisfy longer than the caffeine surge from a cup of coffee.

There is something more.

I'm guessing you have a Bible somewhere in your home. Go get it. If you don't, put down this book and download the free Bible app on your phone. We have access to God's Word—living water poured out through ink on paper. This gift is yours and mine for the soul strengthening. Nothing can quench our thirst like God's Word.

We can make spending time with God feel too complicated. It doesn't have to be hard. You don't have to wake up an hour before your kids and light a candle and sit in peaceful solitude in order for Scripture to be a meaningful part of your motherhood. (If you can do an extended morning quiet time in the season you're in, that's fantastic! What a beautiful gift!) But if all you can muster is five minutes while you're giving the baby her morning bottle or three minutes in the car line at school pickup, start there. You could begin in James or with one of my favorite verses in Psalms: "Teach me your way, Lord, that I may rely on your faithfulness" (Psalm 86:11).

Teach me Your way, Lord. Teach me Your way.

Make it your prayer for today. Recite it when you're making mac 'n' cheese and rewashing the mildewy towels.

When you feel right wrung out, God is ready to fill your cup. Your emptiness is not something to be ashamed of or quick-fixed. It's part of the motherhood gift . . . pointing you to Him.

. . . .

one simple step

Choose one to practice today.

☐ Practice recognizing the Holy Spirit speaking to you. Look back at the four-bullet list earlier in the chapter. Examine a strong thought or feeling with those guiding questions in mind.

☐ Where in motherhood do you feel most depleted? Talk honestly with God about your struggles. Ask Him to meet you in that place.

☐ Write Psalm 86:11 on a sticky note and put it on your fridge, computer, or bathroom mirror. "Teach me your way, LORD, that I may rely on your faithfulness." Recite it every time you see it.

. . . .

one powerful prayer

Make this your daily prayer.

Jesus, I love being a mom, but I get so thirsty from pouring out so much of myself. Thank You for being the giver of living water. Teach me what it means to be filled up in You. I don't want to stay empty when I could feast on Your Word of truth. I'm ready. Lead the way. Amen.

ten

The Beauty of Being Handpicked

Today was a typical morning. Before seven o'clock, Elias was asking a hundred questions about earthquakes and Minecraft and housing prices while insisting on assembling every piece of the percolator I just cleaned. He spilled coffee grounds all over the counter. Noah was outside in his pajamas hunting crickets. Jude was still buried in his mountain of stuffed animals, pretending he didn't notice that I turned off the nightlight, opened the curtains, and rubbed his back.

Eventually all three boys ate their frozen waffles, threw away their paper plates (yep, I'm that kind of mama), and returned their barely sipped milk cups to the fridge. Each boy put on their shoes and brushed their teeth, and two out of three combed their hair. They even put away the individual piles of laundry I folded and stacked last night while watching an episode of *Friends* on Netflix.

None of their morning jobs were done perfectly or without half-a-dozen reminders to *focus* and *stay on task*. But you guys! They did it! Do you know what this means?

This means I HAVE SURVIVED! I no longer have a house full of littles. Gone are the bottle-warming, spoon-feeding, diaper-changing, must-be-supervised-ninety-eight-percent-of-the-time days! I no longer worry that silence in the back of the house could mean that someone stuck their finger in an electrical outlet or choked on a marble. And if *I* can survive the longest-fast phase of motherhood, then *for sure* you can too.

Today my not-babies-anymore babes climbed into the minivan, strapped themselves in, then unbuckled and filed out when we reached the school drop-off circle. Elementary school, people! Where my kids are loved, supervised, taught, encouraged, and guided by trained adults *who are not me* for 351 minutes of the day. Not that I'm counting.

"Love you, Mom!" Elias said and leaned across the second-row seat to give me a kiss despite throwing an attitude five minutes earlier because I let Jude use his booster seat.

"Love you, boys! Be kind and loving and have a good day!" I called as the van door slid shut. *Hallelujah.* A Monday morning victory without even brushing my hair.

If this little scene seems like a big-screen fairytale, a *wouldn't that be nice* dream that will never be your reality, then you, dear mama, are still in the thick of the little years. If that's you, this is what I want you to hear: The season you're in today will not always be this way. Let this fuel your gratitude for what is and your hope for what is to come.

If you had a morning similar to mine, then you're a few steps farther along on your motherhood journey, which makes me raise my almond-milk latte to you in celebratory solidarity. Boom, mama! You survived and are here to tell the tale. We know that this season of school-age kids has its own brand of crazy blessings and challenges. (This afternoon when it's 94 degrees, I will attempt to shepherd three kids through homework, reading, and dinner in the midst of three consecutive soccer practices for three different teams, returning home with just enough time for the stinky men-children to kick off their reeky cleats, shower, and go to bed. *Hold me, Jesus.*)

But we can't let this current season of extracurricular activities and Common Core math cause us to forget how far we've come! If you didn't deal with projectile body fluids today, then you're doing pretty well. But as a mom of older kids, you still have plenty of opportunities to cling to Jesus! Amen? Remember that God is your strength when you're in the middle of tutoring struggling readers, deodorizing shin guards, and figuring out how to satisfy the bottomless pit of growing kids without blowing your grocery budget. At the same time, find a mama with a baby on her hip and cheer her on!

After taking my kids to school, I usually go home and make myself breakfast, rinse away bloated Cheerios left in the kitchen sink, and check email before transitioning to work mode for my job as the community manager for DaySpring's (in)courage. But today, as the boys grabbed their backpacks, I pulled on a clean pair of yoga pants and slid my laptop in my brown leather tote. Then I drove straight from school drop-off to The Coffee Bean & Tea Leaf. To write. To you.

As I settled in at my favorite round table against the left wall, I noticed a mom and her baby seated in the corner. Morning sun was streaming in through the wall of windows, lighting up the wispy hairs that adorned the baby girl's head. The mom had an extra-large iced-something-delicious and bounced the baby on one knee between sips. A large diaper bag with gray and white polka dots took up the rest of the little table. The pair didn't look unhappy. It seemed like they were doing pretty well to be dressed and out of the house by eight. Seemed like a good way to start the day.

Without warning, a lump rose in my throat from somewhere deep inside me and my eyes filled with tears. Why? Because I know appearances never tell the whole story.

I had a sudden impulse to run past the sugar-and-cream station and embrace that mama stranger. I wanted to look her in the eyes and ask how she's *really* doing, ask her to tell me her story. I wanted to celebrate the latest adorable thing her baby learned to do and nod along when she shared the struggle that is keeping her neck in knots at night. I wanted to lean in close and tell her that I'm writing a book for mamas, for *her*. And that maybe she comes here every Monday morning, or maybe we both just happened to be here today so that I could tell her that whether she is truly fine or desperately floundering, whether she's living her dream or living through pain, confusion, or just sheer exhaustion—whatever is beneath the sweet caffeine and bouncing knee—God sees her.

I wish I could tell you that I did those things. That I risked the social awkwardness for the chance to encourage a fellow traveler on this motherhood adventure. But I didn't. I stayed behind my glowing screen, cursor blinking as I blinked back tears. By the time I gathered enough gumption (and composure) to go over, she was gone.

Why did a stranger evoke such raw emotion? I mean, I see moms and babies every day. Around my neighborhood, at the park, school, church, baseball practice, wandering the aisles at Target. So why was I so weepy on a Monday morning?

I can think of two good reasons.

First, digging into my motherhood archives for this book— pulling out forgotten (and purposefully suppressed) memories from my first decade on this mom job—has flooded me with a renewed wonder for how miraculous and grueling it is to be a mother.

I am overwhelmed by the gift of my sons. That I have had the privilege of knowing them since they took their first breath. I'm the one who heard their first deep-belly giggle. I saw Noah's awe-filled eyes on our first neighborhood walk as he strained to turn his infant neck to see every cloud and tree. I was there when Elias finally sat up unassisted, in hand-clapping victory after months of his extra-large noggin toppling him over. I was the one who could differentiate Jude's hunger and tired and wet-diaper cries even with toddler brothers causing a ruckus. And every morning, I was the one who got to see each of my babies' round faces light up with delight; I got to hear the thump, thump of motor legs in

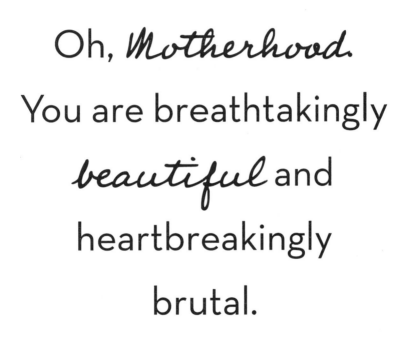

Oh, *Motherhood.*
You are breathtakingly
beautiful and
heartbreakingly
brutal.

footy pajamas kicking with excitement—all because their mama walked into the room.

I was also the one who dealt with nearly every public meltdown and nap-time battle. It was my arms that sometimes couldn't provide enough comfort through the colic, or my breast not enough nourishment through the growth spurt. I got to listen to the car-seat-buckling screeching, deal with the won't-get-dressed back-arching, and see the willful disobedience every ordinary Tuesday afternoon. My shirt has been soaked in hot angry tears from a thrashing toddler who can't control his emotions. I've caught vomit in my hands, and I've cleaned diarrhea out of someone's most-favorite-you-can't-throw-them-away Spider-man chonies.

And I'm guessing you have too.

Oh, Motherhood. You are breathtakingly beautiful and heart-breakingly brutal. You are the highest honor and greatest challenge I have ever been given. One minute you make me want to weep, and the next throw my head back and dance in a whirlwind of painful, extravagant grace.

Since I don't dance in public, I guess stifled weeping over my steamy latte will have to do.

In Good Company

My long and lingering stroll down memory lane to extract stories for this book leads to the second reason a coffee-shop stranger evoked so much early-morning emotion: God is answering my prayer.

Over the last many weeks as I've been writing, I've asked God to give me a supernatural love for you, the women who would read *No Better Mom for the Job*. When I'm struggling with my own inadequacy, I pray for every mom who finds herself in a similar place. I pray that every word I write would be a reflection of God's fierce love for His daughters. And that every mom who reads this book would feel like a friend is hugging her page by page, cheering her on to keep on keeping on.

I pray this is how you've felt. I pray you are starting to know deep in your soul and to the marrow of your bones that you are called and equipped as exactly the right mom your kid needs. There is no one better than you to love and raise your child. Whether you have one biological son or three adopted daughters or a blended tribe of ten, you have what it takes!

Just think of the woman God chose to mother His one and only Son. Oh, sweet Mary. Just a teenager. Engaged but not yet officially married. From the outside, there wasn't much that made her look especially qualified to be the mother of God's Son. Of *all* the women God could have chosen, why did He land on one who was so inexperienced? Did He just look at the prophecies and think, this girl will do—she's a virgin with the right lineage, headed to the right town of the promised Messiah's birth? I don't think so. I think God saw something in Mary's heart, something in her character, in who she was or who she was becoming, that made her the right mom for Jesus—just like He saw something in me and in *you* that makes us the right mom for our kids too.

I love thinking about Mary as Jesus' mom and how imperfect her motherhood must have looked. To start, the timing was all wrong. To the world she was an unwed young woman, pregnant, bringing shame to her family and fiancé. Immaculate conception isn't exactly something you can write on a yard sign to explain your circumstances to judgmental neighbors. Nor is it the smoothest way to transition into marriage.

Later Mary had at least one very public mothering blunder. Nothing too big. Ya know, just *losing her son* on a family trip. If that's not a comfort to any mom whose kid has wandered off in Target or gone temporarily missing at a big family party—"I thought Johnny was with *you!*"—I don't know what is.

Can you imagine the adrenaline frenzy Mary must have felt? Not only had she lost *her* son, she had lost *God's* Son! And it wasn't a quick, *Oh, I found Him under the slide* or *He was hiding inside the closet* kind of thing. They had to go back to Jerusalem, and it took them THREE DAYS to find Jesus. Of course, Mary and Joseph eventually located Him safe and sound, sitting in the temple courts among the teachers, listening to them and asking questions.

I can almost hear Mary's internal dialogue during those three long, searching days. *How could I have let this happen? Why did God make me Jesus' mom? Surely someone else would have been more qualified for the job! Someone wiser, more attentive, more discerning, more organized for goodness' sake! If I would have had my checklist in place and implemented a better buddy system, this never would have happened. What if God made a mistake in choosing me?*

Haven't we all felt that way at one time or another? If only I was more of this or less of that, I could have avoided that serious crisis or embarrassing incident, that public meltdown or pee-on-my-friend's-floor accident. We think someone else would have been better equipped to handle our unique kid—I imagine even the most famous mother of all time did.

But God didn't choose Mary for her perfection. She was just as human and flawed as you and me and probably got PMS sugar cravings and pimples too. God saw something deeper in Mary that made Him say, *Yes, she's the one. Her wiring and personality, her faith and perseverance, her compassion and sense of humor, that's what this child needs. She won't get it perfect, but I don't expect her to. All I need is for her to trust Me to help her for the rest of this child's life.*

He says the same about you.

I'm sure losing Jesus after Passover wasn't the first or last time Mary fumbled through motherhood. I don't know if she held on to any mom guilt or if she struggled with comparison to other moms. But we do know that she was a woman willing to learn through her circumstances.

When they finally found Jesus hanging out in the temple courts, having some good ol' theological conversations, Mary didn't hesitate to express her, umm, displeasure. "When his parents saw him, they were astonished. His mother said to him, 'Son, why have you treated us like this? Your father and I have been anxiously searching for you'" (Luke 2:48).

Jesus turned the question back, expecting His earthly parents to know that He was meant to be in His heavenly Father's house of worship. Despite Jesus not understanding, Scripture says that "his mother treasured all these things in her heart" (Luke 2:51). Mary was willing to learn, to seek God, to store up that which He was doing in her midst. "And Jesus grew in wisdom and stature, and in favor with God and man" (Luke 2:52).

Now, I'm not trying to equate our make-a-run-for-it cherubs with the Son of God. Surely the boy Jesus was unlike any child to ever walk the earth. And His mom was one-of-a-kind too. But what we see through Jesus' life is God's highest esteem for mothers.

I suspect Mary didn't softly ask the question, "Son, why have you treated us like this?" in a syrupy-sweet tone. I hear an edge. Frustration. Perhaps anger on the verge of tears. I also hear her deep, deep care. That's who we are as mothers.

Whether our kids are ten months or twelve years (like Jesus was then), or even twenty-two, we care intensely. We mother fiercely. We are tender and determined. We are our kids' best advocate and cheerleader. We nurture and nourish, listen to and lead, inspire and encourage our children like no one else can. Of course God would choose that kind of love for His Son! He could have chosen a million different ways to deliver the Savior to the world. Lightning bolt, fluffy cloud, blazing chariot storming through the sky. But God chose the messy, painful, awe-inspiring way of human delivery. Christ's earthly body knit together in a mother's womb. His earthly rearing entrusted to a mother's care.

God is intentional. He is purposeful.

Whether you said yes to motherhood through fostering or adopting, caring for your grandchild, nephew, or niece, whether you carefully planned your baby's conception or your little one's arrival was the most unplanned thing you've ever experienced—God chose you! You weren't a roll of the dice or the short straw that got drawn. For such a time as this, for however long the scope of your mothering lasts, *you* are the right mom for the job.

Did God need perfection from Jesus' earthly parents? Nope. Mary's fumbles and blunders didn't thwart God's plans. So you can bet your last pack of wipes He doesn't require perfection from you either. What He requests is also what He offers—confidence. Not confidence in our own abilities, but confidence in His sovereignty.

You cannot parent with confidence by your own careful planning, cutting-edge strategies, or organic-smoothie strength. Your confidence must come from God's with-ness.

Navigating Uncharted Territory

To me, sometimes motherhood feels like a version of the Promised Land. All this beauty and goodness stands before me wrapped up in uncharted territory. There will be untold blessings and riches, but also giants to conquer and wars to wage. And I'm there like Joshua, standing at the edge of the Jordan River, being charged to do something way beyond my own capacity.

When Joshua found out it was up to him to lead God's people into the Promised Land, he must have had a massive lump in his throat. There was so much at stake. *What if I don't have what it takes?* Joshua must have thought. The biblical text doesn't tell us exactly what Joshua said or did, but from what the Lord says to him, we can be pretty sure Joshua was grappling with feelings of inadequacy.

So how did God respond? Did He tell Joshua to hurry up and get on with it? Did He wag His mighty finger and command Joshua to remember everything he learned from Moses, warn him not to mess up? No. God told Joshua all the ways He was going to help him and equip him, and most importantly *go with him*. "The Lord himself goes before you and will be with you; he will never leave you nor forsake you. Do not be afraid; do not be discouraged" (Deuteronomy 31:8).

Mama, if you're fresh on the shore of motherhood and the baby years are a shallow tide lapping at your feet, God is with you!

If you are wading deep in the weary waters and unsure if you'll ever make it to the other side, God is with you!

If you are in the thick of unknown terrain, and very real dangers and insurmountable barriers feel like they will never give way to a more fruitful life, God is with you!

Motherhood is our Promised Land, which means God is with us. He will not leave us.

When the needs in front of us feel too great, when the hope before us seems too far away, God is here. He is near. That is a promise we can cling to when everything else in life gives way. Potty-training charts and expert advice may fail. Your kid might regress, and at some point there will be emotional distress. But you are never alone.

This is also one of the final promises Jesus made.

After Jesus was crucified, buried, and raised to life, He appeared to His closest friends, His disciples. In Jesus' farewell instructions to the Eleven, He first laid out the work they were to do. I love the way *The Message* says it: "Go out and train everyone you meet, far and near, in this way of life. . . . Then instruct them in the practice of all I have commanded you" (Matthew 28:19). Then comes the promise: "I'll be with you as you do this, day after day after day, right up to the end of the age" (Matthew 28:20).

As moms, we don't have to go very far to find someone to train and instruct. Day after day after day, night after night after night, we do the work of motherhood. *I'll be with you as you do this*, Jesus is saying. *I am with you.*

When I wipe my tears and boil it all down, that's really what I want to say to Coffee Bean mom with the polka-dot diaper bag. *God is with you. God is with you. God is with you.*

Tonight, my youngest two would not settle down before bed. They were laughing and fighting and being silly as kids do, but in the process, they were ignoring every word I said. After several attempts to guide and direct them in their bedtime tasks, I told them clearly that if they didn't obey and do the specific things I asked (hard stuff like getting on jammies and going pee) they would lose me for bedtime.

Sure enough, my little bear cubs paused their roughhousing but a breath long enough to feign listening, then jumped right back into their wild antics. Though my inner temperature was rising, I calmly (this time) said, "I'm sorry, guys; you chose not to obey so you've lost Mommy tonight."

Cue the wailing.

Suddenly they were the sorriest ever, and *could we please just have one more chance?* Eyes grew red and little chests heaved and crocodile tears rolled like wet boulders down pouty cheeks. *How could I do this to them?* they sobbed as I brushed their teeth. Keep in mind, "losing me" simply meant that their dad, whom they adore, would tuck them into bed instead.

After a few minutes, Elias came to me blowing his snotty nose and asked, "Mommy, instead of losing you, can I lose my iPad turn or fidget spinner tomorrow? Because those are just toys, and I really want you to sing and pray for me."

Though my heart was melted mush, Chris and I have decided that consequences are not up for negotiation. Sigh. "Not this time, buddy," I said.

As I walked to tuck in Noah, who still got me, Chris called me into the other bedroom and said each boy could have one hug and kiss from me.

As I bent down to cuddle Elias, he pulled my face close, looked into my eyes, and said: "Mommy, your beauty keeps me awake at night."

You guys! This is the beautiful-grit, undone-by-it, wouldn't-trade-it, achy joy of motherhood! This is why we have to stay tender through the tough battles. This is why we have to delight in our kids even when we feel defeated. This is the holy privilege, the store-in-your-heart-forever, laugh-out-loud, and squeeze-them-so-tight glory of raising kids.

This is the hardest, most humbling most uplifting job on the planet. This is the job you were made for.

When you mother, no one is as beautiful as you.

. . . .

one simple step

Choose one to practice today.

☐ Do you need someone to ask how you're *really* doing today? Call a friend and bravely share your heart. Or take five quiet minutes and journal your feelings as a prayer to God.

☐ Think back to a time you felt like you totally blew it as a mom. What can you learn from that situation? How did God meet you in it? Purpose to "store it all up in your heart" like Mary did.

☐ Look for an opportunity to encourage another mom. Tell her she's doing a great job. Remind her that God sees her.

. . . .

one powerful prayer

Make this your daily prayer.

Jesus, thank You for choosing me to be the mom of my kid. Thank You for promising to equip me and walk with me every step of this crazy motherhood journey. I'm exactly the right mom for the job! I can trust that. I trust You. And I love You. Thank You for loving me too. Amen.

Acknowledgments

This book has my name on the cover, but the words on each page wouldn't be possible without a huge team of people.

To the one who first made me a mother: Noah, I am so proud of the responsible young man you are. You are smart, fearless, and kind. It is my greatest delight to watch you grow, cuddle on the couch, and beat you in cards. I'm so grateful I'm your mom.

To my middle boy: Elias, you are one of a kind! With your sparkly eyes and determined strength, you can do anything you set your mind to. You are tender, creative, and curious. I love spending time with you and seeing you explore the world around you. I'm so grateful God made me your mom.

To my baby: Jude, you are the unexpected light we didn't know our family needed. You are silly and caring and the very best friend to many. Your kind heart and respect for others will serve you well in every life season. Let's hold hands while we hike and take Sunday naps together forever. I'm so grateful God gave me you.

To my husband: Chris, you have been a steadfast supporter of my gifts and dreams. How did I get so lucky? Thank you for every hour you gave me to write and edit, taking on more responsibility at home so I could be free to lean into this new work. You are an amazing father—truly—which makes me a better mom. This book wouldn't exist without you. Thank you for loving me so well.

To my editor: Jeff, you have been a phenomenal partner on this publishing journey. Only God could have written the plot of how we connected. Thank you for believing in me and the message of this book even before it was fully formed. I'm indebted to your kindness and talent. *Jeff Braun for president.*

To the entire Bethany House team: Thank you for investing your creativity and expertise to help birth this book baby into the world. Every author needs a team like you.

To my agent: Rachel Kent, thank you for understanding the impact of this message and being the first to say you need this book.

To my professor: Dr. Joseph Bentz, thank you for making me ask the question, "What is possible for me as a writer?" Your encouragement and mentorship made all the difference.

To my Foreword writer: Lisa-Jo, thank you for lending your voice to the pages of this book. You were my motherhood and writing mentor long before we ever met. Thank you for being a fierce champion of mothers! No one deserves a superhero cape more than you.

To my mom: Patty, thank you for loving me and my spirited, particular, amazing crew. I am deeply grateful for all the ways you made time and space to support me in writing this book. You are a truth speaker, a prayer warrior, and the best tuna-melt maker. I love you.

To my dad: I know you would have been proud of me for writing this, and you would've loved knowing the three incredible kids who call me mama. We'll see you again soon.

To my in-loves: Pat and Lelia, thank you for loving our family well and supporting the work God has called me to do.

To my come-alongside friends: Sara, Audra, Desiree, and Kyan, you watched my kids and cheered me on. Your tangible support gave this book wings. I'm so grateful to do life with you.

To my champion-and-cheerlead friends: Mindy, Elise, Tracy, Anjuli, Stephanie, Dorina, Wendy, Kimberlee, Esther, and Rachel, you held me up with your bold prayers, meaningful questions, and fountains of truth poured out over me. My heart needed each of you. What treasures you are from our faithful Father.

To the (in)courage staff: Joy, Anna, and Grace, I'm a better woman and mother because of the privilege of working with you. Don't ever leave your seat on the bus!

To the (in)courage contributors: Thank you for being a safe place to ask questions and lean into the Lord together. You make me a better friend and writer.

To the Build a Sister Up community: You have taught me what it looks like to truly build one another up and link arms for the sake of the kingdom. Grace ninjas forever!

To my favorite connecter: Amber, thank you for making one of the most impactful introductions of my life. I love the way you are *for* others.

To my Cornerstone MOMS team: You girls know how to love well, serve joyfully, and pray fiercely. You are the most beautiful group of mamas I know. It's an honor to walk it all out with you.

And to you, dear reader. I hope you know how proud I am of you. Thank you for trusting me enough to open this book and, in doing so, open the pages of your own motherhood story and faith journey. You are the heartbeat of this message. There's no better mom for the job than *you*!

At one time, I wondered if motherhood would be a barrier to my long-held dream of being a writer. Only God could have known that motherhood would be the very thing that unlocked my dormant passion, helped me connect deeply with Him in the thick of the little years, and set me on a path of ministering to other women. Jesus, You are my Savior, my Guide, and my most trusted Friend. You swung wide the doors for this book. *Thank-You* gets caught in my throat. The words aren't enough. But You know my heart. Buckets of gratitude. You keep filling me up.

Becky Keife is the community manager for DaySpring's (in)courage, a vibrant online community of Christian women. (in)courage provides meaningful resources that help authentic, brave women connect deeply with God and others. In addition to leading the many contributors to this ministry, Becky speaks regularly to MOPS (Mothers of Preschoolers) groups and at other women's events. Encouraging the hearts of women face-to-face is pretty much her favorite. Becky is a huge fan of Voxer, Sunday naps, and moms in the thick of it. She and her husband live near Los Angeles, where they enjoy hiking sunny trails with their three spirited sons.

· ·

❑ Join the No Better Mom community on Instagram @ beckykeife.

❑ Stay connected with Becky at www.beckykeife.com.

❑ Download your free No Better Mom for the Job Discussion Guide at NoBetterMomBook.com.